Mountain Biking
NEAR BOSTON

Fifth Edition - Updated, Revised, Expanded

Mountain Biking
NEAR BOSTON

A Guide to the Best 35 Places to Ride

by Stuart Johnstone
photographs by the author

Active
PUBLICATIONS

Trails and conditions will change over time, so we would appreciate hearing corrections that you find. Your opinions and suggestions are also welcome. Please address them to:

Active Publications
P.O. Box 1037
Concord, MA 01742-1037

Copyright © 1990, 1991, 1994, 1996, 1999 by Stuart A. Johnstone

Published by:
    Active Publications, P.O. Box 1037, Concord, MA 01742-1037

Printed in the United States of America

Publisher's Cataloging in Publication Data

Johnstone, Stuart A.
    Mountain Biking Near Boston: A Guide to the Best 35 Places to Ride / by Stuart A. Johnstone; photographs by the author.
        5th edition, revised
        ISBN 0-9627990-5-X
        1. All-terrain cycling - Massachusetts - Guidebooks.
2. Massachusetts - Description and travel
        Library of Congress Catalog Card Number: 90-85109

This book is dedicated to all who have helped to establish public lands and multi-use trails.

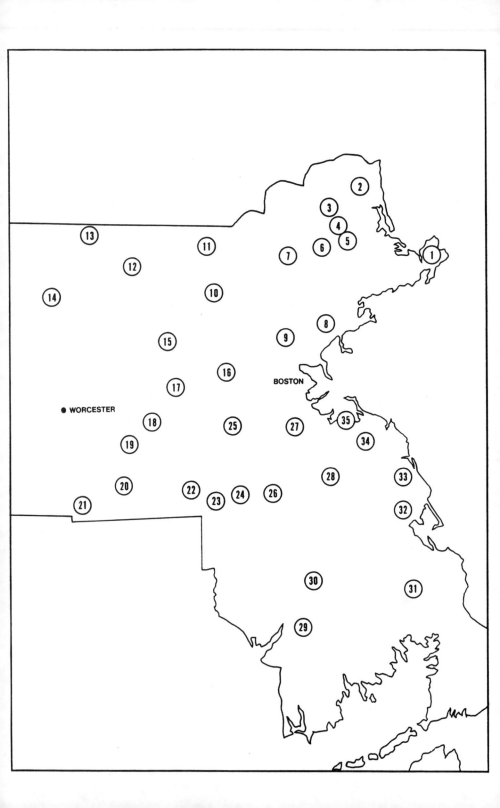

Contents

Introduction

Mountain Biking Near Boston

You don't need pavement in order to ride a bike. And you don't need car traffic, noise, and exhaust fumes either. More people of all ages are discovering the undeniable satisfaction of pedaling along a trail, whether they be out for an easy ride on a gentle forest road or a difficult workout on a challenging single-track. They appreciate the benefits of riding the most durable and versatile bikes ever made, the fun that outdoor exercise brings, and the natural relief of being in the woods.

Fortunately, the Boston area is blessed with a large and growing collection of public lands and trails. Its rolling hills and dales are home to countless miles of riding preserved in one of the country's largest state park systems and a wealth of locally owned properties. Choices in terrain and scenery suit the needs of every pedaler from beginner to expert and range from the remoteness and solitude of distant parklands to the convenience of escape routes close to the city.

Mountain Biking Near Boston has two objectives. The first is to describe each location and its trails for bicyclists by providing difficulty ratings, directions, and loop mileages, information that is important when selecting an area or trail to ride. Aspects of natural and historical background are also included. The second is to communicate the rules and regulations governing the use of bicycles at various parklands and to educate riders about standards of trail etiquette. Since each of the 35 locations has its own combination of rules and conditions for mountain biking, it is hoped that readers will gain an appreciation for the region's public lands and be able to plan rides accordingly.

Trail Manners

Trail access for mountain biking, especially in high use areas close to Boston, is threatened by careless riding habits. Complaints from both land managers and other trail users concerning soil erosion, safety, noise, and other preventable problems have closed trails to mountain bikers in the past and can do so in the future. All cyclists must realize the importance of coexisting in the trail community if the sport of mountain biking is to continue to thrive and, to this end, the International Mountain Biking Association (IMBA) has adopted the following guidelines:

IMBA Rules of the Trail

1. Ride on open trails only. Respect trail and road closures (ask if not sure), avoid possible trespass on private land, obtain permits and authorization as may be required. Federal and state wilderness areas are closed to cycling.

2. Leave no trace. Be sensitive to the dirt beneath you. Even on open trails, you should not ride under conditions where you will leave evidence of your passing, such as on certain soils shortly after a rain. Observe the different types of soils and trail construction; practice low-impact cycling. This also means staying on the trail and not creating any new ones. Be sure to pack out at least as much as you pack in.

3. Control your bicycle! Inattention for even a second can cause disaster. Excessive speed maims and threatens people; there is no excuse for it!

4. Always yield trail. Make known your approach well in advance. A friendly greeting (or bell) is considerate and works well; startling someone may cause loss of trail access. Show your respect when passing others by slowing to a walk or even stopping.

Anticipate that other trail users may be around corners or in blind spots.

5. Never spook animals. All animals are startled by an unannounced approach, a sudden movement, or a loud noise. This can be dangerous for you, for others and for the animals. Give animals extra room and time to adjust to you. In passing, use special care and follow the directions of horseback riders (ask if uncertain). Running cattle and disturbing wild animals is a serious offense. Leave gates as you found them, or as marked.

6. Plan ahead. Know your equipment, your ability and the area in which you are riding -- and prepare accordingly. Be self-sufficient at all times. Wear a helmet, keep your machine in good condition, and carry necessary supplies for changes in weather or other conditions. A well-executed trip is a satisfaction to you and not a burden or offense to others.

Specific concerns regarding the heavily used trails of eastern Massachusetts deserve emphasis. Most importantly, never ride on a trail when conditions are wet (either from rain or from spring thaw) since soils erode easily during these times. Keep to well-drained gravel roads in spring until mud season has past, which is typically mid-April in the Boston area but often later at other locations. Land managers point out that all forms of trail use lead to erosion and that visitors should focus on minimizing this damage.

When crossing streams, especially those with silty or muddy bottoms, dismount your bike and walk across to prevent unnecessary disruption. When crossing puddles or mudholes it is best to either ride or walk through the center rather than to circle the edge and cause the trail to widen. Since every situation is different, use your judgement and choose the least disruptive course.

Never skid! Not only does it disturb the soil surface but it also leaves a visible, negative image for other trail

users. Large group sizes and loudness are also discouraged because they can detract from the outdoor experience of others, so limit group sizes whenever possible and respect the peace and quiet of the woods.

Realize that horses are easily frightened by mountain bikes. With relatively poor eyesight and only *flight or fight* instincts, they are prone to panic when a bike approaches quickly and quietly, creating a potentially dangerous situation. Upon meeting a horse, bicyclists should come to a complete stop at the side of the trail and make verbal contact with the rider well in advance so that the animal will feel safe. Sometimes dismounting the bike will also be helpful. Especially when approaching from behind, wait for the equestrian's instructions before proceeding.

Pedaling softly means riding on trails in a way that allows you to return to them another day. Be sensitive to the soil surface beneath you, remember the concerns of a hiker at a blind corner, and understand that trails are a limited and valuable resource. Educate others about good riding habits and the importance of preventing trail closures, and protect the future by demonstrating that mountain bikes can be ridden safely with minimal impact on the environment.

Volunteer!

Give back to the trails. Volunteer your time, effort, and/or money for the benefit of the trails that you ride and discover the powerful satisfaction that comes from trail stewardship. The Boston area is fortunate to have the force of the New England Mountain Bike Association (NEMBA) providing organized volunteer opportunities for both trail maintenance and trail patroling, in addition to group rides and annual festivals. The efforts of NEMBA volunteers have left a great impression on numerous Boston area park managers in recent years and the future for more work, and fun, is limitless. Get in touch with your local NEMBA chapter to learn more: (800) 57-NEMBA or www.nemba.org.

Trail Policies

Banned from many of the country's public lands, mountain biking is not an acceptable activity on every trail. While bicyclists are welcomed in most of the Boston area's parklands, restrictions usually exist and it is important to understand and respect them. A few areas simply do not permit any mountain biking. Since different land managers across the state have different concerns and perspectives, rules and regulations concerning mountain biking vary from place to place. They also change with time so be alert for trailhead notices regarding current trail policies.

Massachusetts state parks and forests are administered by the Dept. of Environmental Management and follow a set of state-wide rules for mountain biking. According to the policy, bicycles are permitted on all trails unless they are posted as being closed. Bicyclists are required to ride in a safe manner, to respect the concerns of other trail users, and to refrain from riding in wet conditions. Riding off any trail is prohibited. Visitors are urged to send their comments and concerns regarding state properties to the Division of Forests and Parks, 100 Cambridge St., 19'th Floor, Boston, MA 02202, Tel. (617) 727-3180, or visit the website at www.state.ma.us/dem.

Metropolitan District Commission reservations offer 15,000 acres of public property within Boston's metropolitan area. Given their proximity to population, these parks get high levels of use and require cyclists to be extra cautious. Mountain biking is not permitted at any MDC reservation between January 1 and April 15 each year, when trail surfaces are most vulnerable. Groups of more than 6 riders must have a special use permit. Additional restrictions apply at each of the two largest reservations, Blue Hills and Middlesex Fells, and are described in those chapters. For further information contact the MDC at 20 Somerset St., Boston, MA 02108, Tel. (617) 727-1300, web: www.state.ma.us/mdc.

The Trustees of Reservations is the country's oldest land conservation organization and one of the largest private landowners in Massachusetts. Founded in 1891, it has acquired 18,500 acres for public use. Mountain biking is not allowed at these reservations from March 1 through April 30 or during winter months when snow conditions permit cross country skiing. It is permitted only on double-track trails and in groups of 5 or less. Mountain bikers are advised to yield the right of way to other trail users, ride in a safe and responsible manner at all times, and to be alert for additional restrictions at individual properties. Trails closed to bicycling are posted with signs. For further information contact the Trustees of Reservations, 572 Essex St., Beverly, MA 01915, Tel. (978) 921-1944, web: www.thetrustees.org.

Locally owned lands are subject to the rules of the conservation commissions or parks departments of the community. Since each has its own expectations and concerns, be sensitive to the general usage and ride accordingly.

All areas ask that visitors not block trailhead gates when parking because work crews and emergency vehicles always need access.

Planning Your Ride

Getting lost or injured, underestimating trip length or difficulty, and overestimating your own strength or skill level can bring dire consequences in the far reaches of the woods. A weather change or bicycle failure can ruin an otherwise wonderful ride. Be prepared for the worst by bringing some important items.

Drinking water is one of the most essential things to remember. It is easy to become dehydrated while mountain biking because the constant cooling breeze masks the effects of your physical exertion so carry at least one water bottle on the bike frame or in a fanny pack and start drinking before you get thirsty. Many of the longer tours described in this book could require several water bottles, especially in the heat of summer. Water taken from streams should be considered unsafe since it often harbors infectious bacteria such as *Giardia lamblia*, spread when human and animal wastes are deposited near water sources. Be careful not to contribute to the problem.

Even if you are not planning a picnic, bring something to eat in case you body runs low on fuel. A high-energy snack can provide an important boost both physically and psychologically on a long ride.

Carry a map if you are unsure of the trails that you plan to ride and keep track of the route that you follow. Using the mileage directions provided in this book will require a cyclometer, a tiny trip computer that mounts on the handlebars and, operating on a magnetic signal from the front wheel, displays distance, time, speed and other useful information.

Be prepared with bug repellent during spring and summer when mosquitoes and deer flies can create unwanted memories. Consider extra clothing and rain gear since weather changes can occur suddenly. A first-aid kit is also wise. These items add only minimal amounts of weight relative to their potential reward and can be carried either on the body or in a bike pack.

Finally, ride with a companion, especially in remote places where help is far away, and leave word of your destination with a responsible person.

When not to Ride

Mountain biking is discouraged, if not prohibited, at certain times. These include during and immediately after rainy periods and during spring thaw, when the ground is soft and vulnerable to rutting and erosion. In winter during periods of snow cover, mountain bikers are asked to avoid cross country ski trails. And in the late fall (November and December), riding is discouraged Monday through Saturday at many locations when deer hunting season is underway. State law prohibits hunting on Sunday, so that day is considered safe for riding.

Bike Tools

Mountain bikes are built for abuse but still require regular maintenance and repairs, so it is smart to carry some basic tools and to know how to use them. Repairing a flat tire requires either a spare inner tube or a patch kit complete with sanding paper, patches, and glue, along with a pump that can attach securely to the bike's frame. Bring tire irons to help remove the tire from the rim, a small allen wrench/screw driver set to tighten or adjust various bike parts, and a spoke tightener to adjust spokes or remove those that break. A chain tool is necessary to repair chains when links break or bend. All of these tools and supplies can be carried in a small bike pack fitted either under the seat, on the frame, or in front of the handlebars.

Many of the trails described in this book are remote so it is important that your bicycle be well-tuned and properly maintained. If you are not capable of making general repairs on the trail and are not self-sufficient with tools, ride with others who are.

The Equipment

Mountain bikes are available in a large variety of makes and models and a bicycle dealer can best explain the options. The important distinction is between *mountain bike* and *city bike* or *hybrid*, for the two are related but not the same. Mountain bikes have stronger frames, wider tires, and components that are specifically designed for off-road use.

The finely tuned and expensive components on a mountain bike will wear and corrode with use so protect your equipment with routine maintenance. Clean the bike after riding if dirt and sand have accumulated on it because the debris will grind at each moving part and shorten its lifespan. Rinsing the chain, chainrings, and derailleurs with water and applying a bicycle lubricant will usually suffice but sometimes a more serious scrubbing is required. Brake cables, derailleur cables, and even the seatpost should be kept clean and well-greased so that they will remain moveable. Adjust the brake pads as they wear so that they do not rub unevenly or start to touch the tire instead of the rim.

What to Wear

The most important item is a helmet. Comfortable to wear and light in weight, it is considered to be a mountain biker's best friend and valuable protection against the trees, rocks, and other obstacles along the trail. Since three quarters of all bicycle-related deaths result from head injuries, a helmet should be considered a necessity. Protective eyewear is an effective defense from overhanging tree branches.

Nearly anything will do for clothes, but bring enough layers to suit possible weather changes. Bike shorts are a great advantage because the elastic material fits close to the body to eliminate chafing and the padded crotch provides a welcome layer of extra cushion. In colder weather, full-length bicycle pants and a windbreaker/shell are a good match.

Gel-filled gloves are effective at absorbing the bumps and vibrations of the trail and also help prevent numbness in the hands, a common condition for bicyclists. Footwear varies from comfortable hiking shoes to specifically designed mountain biking shoes that physically attach to the bike's pedals.

About the Guidebook

Mountain biking is a sport meant for exploration, and this guidebook is meant to be a stepping stone to that end. It has been written to prepare riders with trail policies, trail descriptions, suggested destinations, and background information. Maps are included to provide a general description of trail networks and natural features, but U.S. Geological Survey topographical maps will be helpful supplements. Note that the map scale for each area varies widely so plan your course accordingly.

Specific terms are used to describe trails. *Single-track* refers to a trail width for just one rider and *double-track* refers to width for two or more bicyclists riding side-by-side. Hiking trails and footpaths are commonly classified as single-tracks and forest roads as double-tracks. Some double-track trails become overgrown with tall grass and weeds in summer so they could appear as single-tracks and, conversely, some single-tracks could appear as double-tracks in winter. Gravel roads signify unpaved routes that are generally passable by car.

A three-grade rating system is used to define levels of trail difficulty. Hills, corners, surfaces, and obstacles such as rocks and logs contribute to this rating. *Easy* applies to routes suitable for beginners with gentle terrain and smooth, open surfaces. *Intermediate* refers to trails with moderate hills and avoidable rocks, roots, and other obstacles. *Difficult* describes those with steep hills and/or rugged, "technical" surfaces. Be careful to select routes that suit your ability and physical strength or be willing to walk the sections that do not.

Practical information accompanies each description. This includes sources of additional information and nearby bike shops for quick access to parts and service. Driving directions originate from major highways and will be most helpful when used together with a road map. Each site has only the major parking areas displayed on the trail map so smaller spots could also exist.

Directions for public transportation on commuter rail lines are included when possible. Permits (costing $5 and valid for 3 years) are required to bring bicycles on commuter trains and can be purchased from the MBTA. Bicycles are permitted on trains (at no extra charge) except during weekday rush hour periods, which are shaded on all train schedules, and on certain holidays and days of special events. Contact either the MBTA at (617) 222-3200, www.mbta.com/bikepass.html or MassBike at (617) 542-BIKE, http://www.massbike.org for more information.

Disclaimer

The author and Active Publications bear no liability for accidents, injuries, losses, or damages caused directly or indirectly by people engaged in the activities described in this book. It is the responsibility of every off-road bicyclist to ride with safety and consideration.

Mountain Biking
NEAR BOSTON

A Guide to the Best 35 Places to Ride

1
Dogtown Common
Gloucester

The inland hills of Cape Ann are a forgotten place when compared to nearby coastal attractions, but mountain bikers consider their 30 or so miles of rocky trails to be a worthy destination and one of the Boston area's most challenging playgrounds.

BACKGROUND:

The name *Dogtown* refers to an abandoned village on the property that originated in the early 1700's. It began as a farming community but fell into decline during the Revolutionary War when residents found it more desireable to live by the coast, and by the 1800's the settlement had been abandoned. The dilapidated houses became home to packs of wild dogs, giving the area its name.

Gloucester gained much of this 3,000-acre tract through the generosity of Roger Babson, founder of Babson College in Wellesley, who saw the importance of preserving the area's natural scenery and its water resources.

TRAIL POLICIES:

Since the area is managed as watershed property, strict rules are posted at trailheads to keep the land and water clean. Swimming, hunting, and motorized uses are among the prohibited activities. Passive recreation is encouraged but mountain bikers are asked to be especially sensitive to concerns of erosion on the trails.

ORIENTATION:

Two trailheads provide the main access to Dogtown and both are located along its western bounds, with the trails spreading north and east toward the village of Rockport. A set of railroad tracks that skirts the trail network can be seen, or at least heard, as a useful point of reference to the south and east but few landmarks exist to the north where private bounds can be difficult to distinguish.

Most trails are blazed and named but not marked by signs, and many of the intersection numbers on the map are missing from their designated locations so keep track of your course when exploring for the first time.

DOUBLE-TRACKS:

Dogtown Road was the main street of the village and follows stone walls past former home sites that are now barely identifiable through the brush. It runs eastward from the parking lot for a mile with easy conditions to Dogtown Square, once the village center and now merely an intersection of trails beside overgrowing meadows. Note that the adjoining trails are rocky so easy pedaling here is quite limited.

The Gee Ave. trailhead accesses mellower double-tracks. A 2-mile, paved bicycle loop around Goose Cove Reservoir provides the starting point for the **Common Road** at intersection 3 on the eastern side of the reservoir. It starts with an eroded hill climb where loose rocks make for a tricky ride, then levels with a smoother, firmer surface for most of its 1.2-mile length. A few additional spots have intermediate conditions from loose rocks on eroded slopes but these are short-lived and most of the riding is easy. Near the midpoint look for Peter's Pulpit, a huge, glacial boulder that looms beside the trail.

Intersection 16 marks the end of the Common Road at the **Luce Trail**, a path that varies widely in conditions for biking. Turning left (north) from the Common Road, the trail immediately encounters difficult riding on a rocky slope near the Whale's Jaw, a split boulder formation, then becomes smooth as it approaches intersection 18. Turning right (south) on the Luce Trail yields a smooth surface for another quarter-mile to Briar Swamp, a 200-acre floating bog where a boardwalk permits visitors to observe habitat for many rare plant species including insectivorous pitcher plants. Continuing past intersections 15 and 14, the Luce Trail reduces to single-track and is extremely rocky near the pile

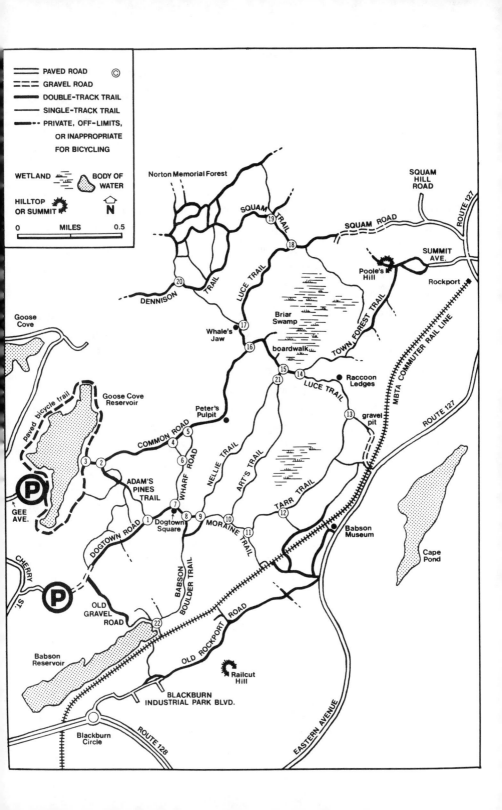

of boulders known as Raccoon Ledges.

Luce Trail ends at intersection 18 at the **Squam Trail**, an extension of Squam Rd. which rises from the village of Rockport. For intermediate riding, turn left and follow the Squam westward to a tangle of trails in the Norton Memorial Forest, a property owned by the New England Forestry Foundation.

Another of Dogtown's various double-tracks is **Old Rockport Road**, a mile-long route between the Blackburn Industrial Park Blvd. and Eastern Ave. Lined with stone walls, it is an easy ride except for a few rocky spots and is mostly downhill when traveled in the west-to-east direction.

SINGLE-TRACKS:

Plenty of gnarly footpaths await intermediate and expert riders eager to hop rocks and test their turning, but note that some are obscure and can easily be missed. **Wharf Road** is relatively easy to spot and provides a useful linkage between Dogtown Square and Common Road with a half-mile of zig-zags between trees and rocks. Bicycle tires can roll smoothly between most of the obstacles so it is an intermediate ride. **Adam's Pines Trail** has a challenging midsection where a rocky slope awaits, but is milder toward each end. The **Moraine Trail** starts at Dogtown Square and gradually becomes narrower and rockier as it drops downhill to the MBTA Commuter Rail Line, then crosses the tracks and continues to Eastern Ave. in flatter terrain. Trains use these tracks frequently, so use caution when crossing.

Both the **Nellie Trail** and **Art's Trail** stretch for a mile between Briar Swamp and the Moraine Trail with extremely difficult conditions. Clogged with rocks, the trails are rideable in only a few sections and require frequent carries.

The **Town Forest Trail** starts from the Rockport area as a smooth jeep road but eventually becomes a boneyard of rocks near Briar Swamp. The adjoining, unnamed single-track circling the northeastern corner of the swamp to the Luce Trail is another tightrope for bikers who must match their balancing skills to a twisted, rocky course. Lasting for a half-mile, it is a difficult, technical ride.

One of Dogtown's most memorable routes is the mile-long **Babson Boulder Trail**, named for Roger Babson who had many of the boulders along the route inscribed with inspirational words like *Truth*, *Integrity*, and *Kindness* and messages like *Help Mother* and *Be On Time*. Although some are obscured by foliage, others sit prominently beside the trail and cannot be ignored. The trail begins in the meadows by Dogtown Square and descends in step-like pitches to Babson Reservoir, turns right and parallels the railroad tracks for a short distance, and then turns left and climbs a steep slope to the endpoint at Blackburn Industrial Park Blvd. It threads a difficult course through a rocky landscape and will be most rideable in the north-to-south (mostly downhill) direction. Linking the Moraine Trail, Old Rockport Road, and Babson Boulder Trail forms an ambitious, 3.3-mile loop from Dogtown Square.

DRIVING DIRECTIONS:

From Rte. 128 exit at Grant Circle and follow Rte. 127 north toward Annisquam. Turn immediately right on Poplar St. then left on Cherry St. and drive for 0.7 miles to Dogtown Rd. on the right or continue to the end of Cherry St., turn right on Gee Ave. and find the reservoir trailhead 0.2 miles ahead at a metal gate.

PUBLIC TRANSPORTATION:

The Rockport Line stops at both Gloucester and Rockport. From the Gloucester station, follow Washington St. north to Grant Circle, then as above. From the Rockport station, turn left on Railroad Ave., then left on Summit Ave. to reach the trails.

BIKE SHOPS:

Harborside Cycle, 48 Rodgers St., Gloucester, Tel. (978) 281-7744

Joe's Bike Shop, 76 Rodgers St., Gloucester, Tel. (978) 283-2552

Seaside Cycle, 23 Elm St., Manchester, Tel. (978)526-1200

ADDITIONAL INFORMATION:

Dogtown Advisory Committee, Community Development, Poplar St., Gloucester, MA 01930

2
Maudslay State Park
Newburyport

Sitting high on a bank above the Merrimack River's final turns, Maudslay State Park is an ideal place for a leisurely ride through a beautiful landscape. Its 10 miles of tree-lined carriage roads have mostly easy mountain biking so kids, elders, and first-timers will feel comfortable exploring the area, and its great scenery affects every trail so visitors should come prepared with a camera, a picnic, or at least plenty of time to stop and gaze.

BACKGROUND:

Purchased by the state in 1985, Maudslay is a relatively new park. It was once the private estate of Newburyport's prosperous Moseley family which began acquiring pieces of this 476-acre tract in the 1800's. Originally known as *Maudsleigh*, the name of the family's ancestral home in England, the estate's main buildings no longer stand but the grandeur of the grounds remains in the landscape of manicured gardens, distinctive trees, and abundant blossoms. A listing of each month's flowering plants is provided at the trailhead bulletin board by the parking lot.

Toilet facilities have been built at the trailhead parking lot and staff are on site to maintain the grounds and assist visitors. The park headquarters is located in a white clapboard house across the street from the parking lot.

TRAIL POLICIES:

Bicycling is permitted only on gravel roads and double-track trails north of the park headquarters building as shown on the accompanying map. Bikes are excluded from all of the park's single-track trails, the gravel roads and double-tracks surrounding the Moseley House Site, Main House Site, and gardens, and all trails south of Curzon's Mill

Rd. Many of the trails that are closed to biking are clearly marked by signs bearing the *no bikes* symbol.

These restrictions are necessary to accommodate the large numbers of visitors and various kinds of trail uses at Maudslay. Especially on weekends, the trails are alive with walkers, joggers, horseback riders, and other bicyclists so keep to slow speeds and be ready to yield the trail. The staff requests that bicyclists stay on established trails and refrain from riding off-trail. Fortunately most routes are open for pedalers to explore and enjoy the park's unique places, and it is hoped that the rules will be respected.

The park is open from 8:00 AM to sunset each day and the parking lot is locked each night so plan your ride accordingly.

ORIENTATION:

Maudslay State Park is not a particularly large area but its tight cluster of trails produces a relatively large number of intersections, which can cause confusion for newcomers. For bicyclists, the trails spread northward from the sole parking lot and are confined by Pine Hill Rd. on the east side and the natural boundary of the river on the west. Few trails lead off the park property to the north. Trail signs are not present so bring the map and follow your progress as you ride.

Mountain biking conditions are easy on the gravel roads and vary between easy and intermediate on the double-track trails.

GRAVEL ROADS:

Begin on the **Pasture Trail** which starts at a break in the stone wall directly across the street from the parking lot and leads to the park's network of mountain biking options. Its gravel surface descends to the left through a hayfield to the shade of woods at **Mile Circle**, a friendly loop road of a slightly shorter distance than its name implies. Flat and smooth, Mile Circle offers beautiful scenery including the Merrimack River, slender **Flowering Pond**, and several

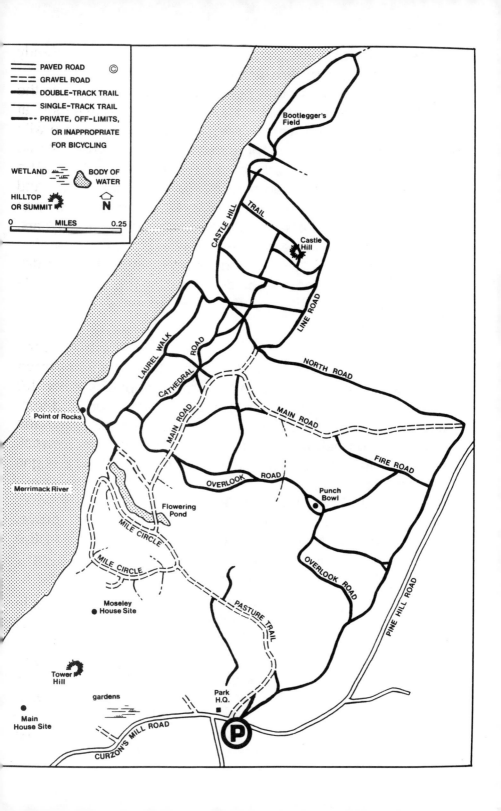

arched, stone bridges.

Mountain bikers are permitted to proceed only northward from this point on **Main Road**, another gravel route which visits some of the park's woodlands, meadows, and rows of shade trees. After crossing the pond on a handsome bridge, it rises through a sloped field where a few loose rocks liven the surface. At the top, the road finds a level course between two hills and enjoys a quarter-mile of shade from an evergreen forest, then emerges at an intersection in another field. Forking right, Main Road follows a row of old trees across the field, climbs a second slope, then returns to the woods and continues for another half-mile before ending beside Pine Hill Rd. Combining Pasture Trail, Mile Circle, and Main Road makes a 1.8-mile ride, one-way.

DOUBLE-TRACKS:

A variety of appetizing double-track trails diverge from Main Road. Although tree roots ripple its surface, **Overlook Road** is an easy ride and explores an undisturbed forest at the edge of a ridgeline where cyclists see glimpses of open fields below. Halfway along is the **Punch Bowl**, a kettlehole formed after the Ice Age by the melting of a huge block of glacial ice.

North Road takes an easy course along the park boundary, passing through a grove of hemlocks on its way from the end of Main Road at Pine Hill Rd. to a four-way intersection where **Line Road** and **Castle Hill Trail** begin. The Castle Hill Trail is recommended for its scenery as it follows the edge of a shelf of land about 100 feet above the river for much of its length. It then turns on a tree-lined course to the top of **Castle Hill**, where there is a view over a surrounding meadow.

Signs posted along parts of the Castle Hill Trail and Main Road warn visitors of a sensitive ecological zone, an area that is closed to all public use between November 1 and March 31 each year. This area extends from Main Road to the Merrimack River between Flowering Pond and

Castle Hill Trail. It is closed to protect both the habitat of migrating bald eagles and a naturally occurring grove of mountain laurel bushes which are vulnerable to human activity during winter. The huge bushes, known to have been thriving here since the 1700's, form a thick barrier on the forest floor and give a unique atmosphere to trails like **Laurel Walk**. Most of the biking along this trail is easy but two short, steep hills are rough with exposed tree roots. Some of the best river views can be enjoyed from the shoreline trail past **Point of Rocks** where a jungle of mountain laurel sits beneath towering white pines. Less-used **Cathedral Road** takes a parallel course high on the hillside above this trail.

A final loop can be made at the park's northern reach in the area known as **Bootlegger's Field**. No longer a field, this stand of red pines sits in a quiet corner of the property with an easy, half-mile ride for mountain bikers. Descending from the Castle Hill Trail, the route crosses an abandoned road which descended from the high bank to the river's edge along a corridor dug deeply into the slope. This road served a ferry which crossed the river here at one time.

DRIVING DIRECTIONS:

From I-95 take Exit 57 and follow Rte. 113 east for a half-mile. Turn left on Noble St., continue to the end, then turn left on Ferry Rd. Bear left at the next fork (continuing on Ferry Rd. which becomes Pine Hill Rd.) and the parking lot is 1.3 miles ahead on the left.

From I-495 take Exit 55 and follow Rte. 110 east for 1 mile. Turn right on Merrill St., cross the bridge over the Merrimack River, then continue straight on Spofford St. At the end turn right on Ferry Rd. and park 1.3 miles ahead on the left.

BIKE SHOPS:

Aries Sports, 96 Route 1, Newbury, Tel. (978) 465-8099
Riverside Cycles, 50 Water St. (The Tannery), Newburyport
Tel. (978) 465-5566

ADDITIONAL INFORMATION:

Maudslay State Park, Curzon Mill Rd., Newburyport, MA 01950, Tel. (978) 465-7223

3
Crane Pond
Wildlife Management Area
Groveland

Crane Pond is unique among most Boston area parks and forests in that it attracts no crowds, offers no facilities, and lies hidden among pot-holed back roads. The area's 20 miles of double-tracks hold easy and intermediate riding.

BACKGROUND:

This 2,300-acre property was established by the federal government in the 1940's and later transferred to the state to be managed as a wildlife area. Hunting remains one of the most popular activities especially during the late fall when the Massachusetts deer season is underway, so mountain biking is not advised during this period except on Sundays, when hunting is prohibited by state law.

Trailhead gates are left open during the main hunting season and as a result many of the trails get used frequently by four-wheel-drive vehicles and are severely eroded and rutted. Unfortunately, given the area's isolation and seldom traveled roads, visitors must also be visually prepared to encounter dump sites of discarded appliances and other refuse.

TRAIL POLICIES:

Crane Pond Wildlife Management Area is overseen by the state's Division of Fisheries and Wildlife. Mountain biking is permitted on all trails but strongly discouraged in the late fall when the deer season is underway and in the early spring when the many low-lying areas will be wet and muddy.

ORIENTATION:

The property covers a large area in the towns of Georgetown, Groveland, Newbury, and West Newbury that is crossed by several public roads. Many of the trails are fragmented in either dead end segments or isolated loops that rely on adjoining public roads for linkage. The centerpiece of the preserve is a large, open wetland containing Crane Pond which serves as a visible landmark from several directions.

The trails do not have signs but the property boundaries are marked by white tree tags. Small parking areas are established at many of the trail/road intersections but only the central lot is displayed on the accompanying map.

DOUBLE-TRACKS:

The backbone of the trail network is **Brown Island Road**, an old county road which traverses the soggy 2 miles between J.B. Little Rd. in Groveland and Crane Neck Hill St. in West Newbury. This road is a favorite of the four-wheel-drive crowd and has been rutted and gauged so severely that much of its surface lies beneath large puddles even in the driest of times. Especially near the midpoint, mountain bikers should plan on getting their feet wet when riding this road end-to-end. Along the way, look for Brown Island to provide both dry ground and a scenic spot to rest.

It is possible to avoid many of these puddles by using adjoining trails like the one beginning at the main parking lot on J.B. Little Rd. Unnamed, this 1.2-mile, intermediate-level trail takes a parallel course on higher ground and eventually ends at Brown Island Road. The first half-mile follows a series of clearings, rolling and turning with a constant flow of small hills, bumping over several rocky areas, and passing numerous dead end side trails, while the second half is forested and a mostly downhill ride.

This unnamed trail forms the first leg of a 4-mile, intermediate-level loop. Follow it for 0.6 miles from the parking lot and then turn left on a double-track heading north into the woods. Wandering for nearly a mile back to J.B. Little Rd., this trail has a remote feeling and explores a wooded landscape of small knolls, granite boulders, and exposed ledge. At the end, cross the road diagonally to the

30

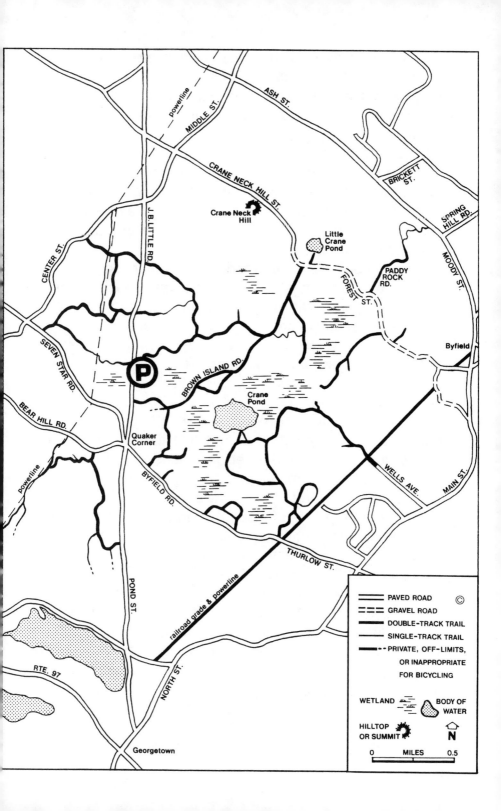

left and find another trail continuing westward, then take the first left and ride south through several meadows and eventually up a sizeable slope. Turn right at the top on a trail that climbs for a short distance, then descends across a set of powerlines, crosses a stream, and emerges at a trailhead off Seven Star Rd. at the 3-mile mark. Turn hard left at this point, descend back to the powerlines and across the stream, then turn right and follow a single-track along a stone wall at the property boundary. This trail widens and becomes rocky in a few spots before returning to J.B. Little Rd. at the parking lot.

Other easy and intermediate double-tracks surround **Crane Pond**. Southeast of the pond is an especially scenic loop that originates at Thurlow St. on one end and Wells Ave. on the other and provides the only direct access to the water. It is less than a mile to reach the pond, which sits amid an open expanse of marsh grass away from any homes, roads, or other signs of civilization.

The **railroad grade and powerline** offer an easy route past this loop between the village centers of Georgetown and Byfield. Straight and flat, the trail has a gravelly surface that is bermed in places from motorcycle usage. A bridge is missing over the Parker River near Forest St. but adjoining roads allow a detour.

Forest St. presents a surprisingly trail-like experience. An unpaved, barely maintained town road, it winds for a mile through rocky, oak forest with a surface cratered with pot holes and puddles. **Little Crane Pond** is visible across another open marsh at the road's western endpoint.

Paddy Rock Road starts from Forest St. with a deceptively easy appearance. The first third of a mile is slowed by only one wet spot, but the remainder of the trail is a trickier affair especially after it reduces to single-track and twists over several small hills, eventually emerging on Moody St. after a total distance of less than a mile.

SINGLE-TRACKS:

Single-track riding is extremely limited at Crane Pond.

The **powerline** corridor near the western boundary has a narrow path offering a challenging course of hills, rocks, and mudholes but it crosses private property at several locations.

A newly-cut single-track off Brown Island Road provides a needed alternative to a puddle-ridden section near the midpoint of the old road. The path begins and ends in relatively flat terrain but tackles a sizeable hill near the midpoint.

DRIVING DIRECTIONS:

From I-95 take Exit 54B and follow Rte. 133 west for 1.9 miles to the traffic signal at Georgetown center. Turn right on North St. and then fork left on Pond St. (which becomes Seven Star Rd. in Groveland) and drive for 1.8 miles. At a 5-way intersection, continue straight on J.B. Little Rd. and look for the parking lot 0.4 miles ahead on the right.

BIKE SHOPS:

Aries Sports, 96 Rte. 1, Newbury, Tel. (978) 465-8099

Riverside Cycles, 50 Water St., Newburyport, Tel. (978) 465-5566

Two for the Road, 74 E. Main St. (Rte. 133), Georgetown, Tel. (978) 352-7343

ADDITIONAL INFORMATION:

Crane Pond Wildlife Management Area, c/o Martin Burns Wildlife Management Area, Box 911, Byfield, MA 01922, Tel. (978) 465-8012

4
Georgetown-Rowley State Forest
Georgetown

Any mountain biker will enjoy this 1100-acre property and its surprisingly secluded 15 miles of trails because the riding includes everything, from single-track to double-track and from easy to difficult.

BACKGROUND:

Little has changed at this state forest over the years. Few signs guide visitors to the obscure trailhead, which is located at the end of a dead-end street, and the parking lot has capacity for only a few cars. No facilities exist except for the trails themselves, and the forest is not staffed. This undeveloped condition lends an solitary flavor to the riding but mountain bikers are not alone on the trails as hikers, off-road motorcyclists, and horseback riders from surrounding farms also share the trails. Hunting is a permitted activity so plan to wear blaze orange during deer season in the late fall.

TRAIL POLICIES:

Georgetown-Rowley is managed by the staff at nearby Bradley Palmer State Park who advise bicyclists to ride at safe speeds and to be alert for other trail users. When approaching hikers and horseback riders, especially from behind, announce your presence well in advance to avoid startling anyone.

The trailhead parking lot is small and is located at two trailhead gates and a private driveway. When parking, be careful not to block access to any of them.

ORIENTATION:

Almost all of Georgetown-Rowley's trails are unnamed, unmarked and devoid of other aids that will direct lost visitors back to the trailhead, so pay careful attention to the map when visiting for the first time. The forest's most visible, and audible, landmark is Interstate 95 which divides the property into two halves, east and west, and allows visitors to judge their location simply by listening for the roar of the traffic.

A bridge for trail users connects the two sides. Most trails lie west of the highway, with the double-tracks being flat and either easy or intermediate riding and the single-tracks being hilly and either intermediate or difficult.

DOUBLE-TRACKS:

The main route through the property is **Pingree Farm Road**, an old wagon road that stretches from Rte. 97 in Georgetown to Rte. 133 in Rowley over a distance of 2.1 miles. Bordered by stone walls, it takes a relatively straight, flat course through woodlands which were once farm fields and offers easy pedaling on a smooth, gravelly surface. Mountain bikers of all abilities will enjoy the ride.

The first half-mile of this road from Rte. 97 is paved. After reaching the trailhead parking area, it continues beyond a brown, metal gate with a dirt surface and a gentle descent, crosses several long straightaways, and then climbs a brief slope at the 1-mile mark. Erosion at this point has left a bumpy surface that livens the pedaling for a short distance. After merging with another double-track, Pingree Farm Road rises on pavement to a bridge that spans Interstate 95's 8 lanes of traffic.

It then descends the other side and enters the eastern half of the forest with a slight downhill slope, bending beneath tall pines and hemlocks with a broader, more gravelly surface. Large puddles, measuring the full width of the road in places, form along this section. The road passes another metal gate at 1.5 miles, arcs around a small hill, then leaves the state forest property and turns northward to reach Rte. 133.

The forest's other double-tracks branch from Pingree Farm Road without names or markings. The easiest ones lie in a cluster to the north and have gentle hills, firm surfaces and the presence of occasional roots and rocks. To the south the trail surfaces are generally rougher, with

36

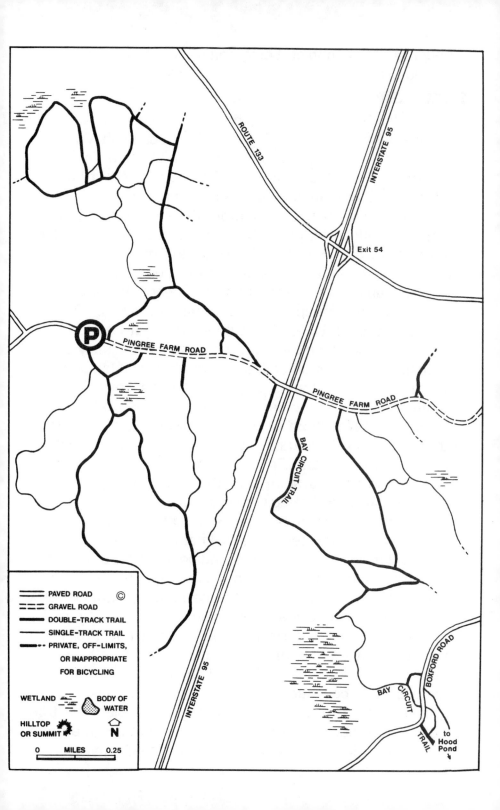

puddles and mudholes being common on the loop east of the highway.

SINGLE-TRACKS:

Nameless, the forest's half-dozen single-tracks tackle steep slopes, corners, and rougher surfaces as they venture off the beaten paths and disappear into the forest's lonelier corners. The gentlest one parallels the western edge of Interstate 95 with an appetizing mix of small rolls and turns.

For a 2.7-mile, intermediate-level ride from the trailhead parking lot on both single- and double-track, take the first left off Pingree Farm Road and ride for a quarter-mile to a single-track on the left heading up a hill. This path skirts a wetland, ascends a long but rideable hill, and finally drops down two steep pitches that can be walked. Turn left at the end on a 0.6-mile double-track that keeps to flat terrain as it bends to the right and almost completely circles a small hill. At the end of this trail turn left, then left again on another 0.6-mile double-track that heads north to circle another hill and then emerges beside a stone wall and field at the forest's northern boundary. Turn right at the end on an old wagon path and ride for a half-mile, then turn right to return to Pingree Farm Road near the parking lot.

Expert riders should try the 2.5-mile loop south of Pingree Farm Road. Begin on the unnamed forest road that forks to the right from its own metal gate at the parking lot. Following the perimeter of the trail network, turn right after a short distance on a single-track and continue for 0.8 miles to the end. Although the treadway is relatively wide for a single-track, a barrage of rocks and constant flow of quick turns and hills make it a challenging ride. Turn right at the end on a double-track that narrows to single-track, rolls with eroded, rocky slopes, and ends after a half-mile at an old wagon road and stone wall near Interstate 95. Turn left at this point and continue for 2 tenths of a mile to the second right turn, another difficult single-track with plenty of tree roots and corners. This half-mile leg ends at Pingree Farm Road; turn left at the end to return to the parking lot.

East of Interstate 95, the white tree tags of the **Bay Circuit Trail** follow the crest of an esker, a glacially created ridgeline, through an area of wetlands on a difficult, 0.8-mile course over tall roots and loose rocks to Boxford Rd. At several points the path ascends and descends this ridge and each is marked by severe erosion since the gravelly soil is relatively unstable. The Bay Circuit, a proposed route circling the Boston area from Newburyport to Duxbury, crosses Boxford Rd. to link the Hood Pond section of neighboring Willowdale State Forest (Chapter 5).

DRIVING DIRECTIONS:

From I-95 take Exit 54B and follow Rte. 133 west for 1.9 miles. At the center of Georgetown, bear left (south) on Rte. 97 and continue for 1.6 miles to Pingree Farm Rd. Turn left and follow the road straight to the end where there is a small parking area. Be careful not to block the gates.

BIKE SHOPS:

The Bicycle Shop, 17 Main St., Topsfield, Tel. (978) 887-6511

Two for the Road, 74 E. Main St. (Rte. 133), Georgetown, Tel. (978) 352-7343

ADDITIONAL INFORMATION:

Georgetown-Rowley State Forest, c/o Bradley Palmer State Park, Asbury St., Topsfield, MA 01983, Tel. (978) 887-5931

5

Willowdale State Forest
Ipswich

Together with neighboring Bradley Palmer State Park, Willowdale offers a 3,000-acre preserve and one of the area's biggest trail systems with over 40 miles of riding. The majority of trails are easy, flat double-tracks that will make any mountain biker feel welcome.

BACKGROUND:

Most of this land was once the private estate of Bradley Palmer, a wealthy Boston lawyer and diplomat who donated his property to the state in the hope that the beautiful scenery could be enjoyed by all. Today it is a haven for fishing, canoeing, picnicking, hiking, horseback riding, and mountain biking. Most of the area's trails were created as bridle paths for Mr. Palmer, an avid equestrian.

Bradley Palmer State Park gets the most visitation with its scenic trails, picnic area, playground, and wading pool, while the expanse of Willowdale State Forest spreads northward for those desiring longer trails and more solitude. Volunteer days are periodically scheduled for trail maintenance; inquire at Bradley Palmer State Park Headquarters if you would like to help.

TRAIL POLICIES:

Mountain biking is permitted on all trails at Willowdale State Forest and Bradley Palmer State Park. Those who manage the property urge mountain bikers to ride in control, to respect other trail users by announcing your presence when approaching, and to pass at a safe speed. These trails are deep in horse country so expect a bumpy ride from hoof prints in places and remember that horses are easily frightened by bicycles. Be ready to stop your bike well in advance, listen for instructions, and offer a few friendly words to help the horse feel at ease.

Hunting is permitted in the western portion of Willowdale State Forest so mountain biking is not advised there in the late fall during deer season, except on Sundays when hunting is prohibited by state law.

Willowdale State Forest consists of two separate blocks of land, one east and the other west of Rte. 1, that are connectable by less than a mile of road. To the east, the larger Pine Swamp area contains the most trails and abutts Bradley Palmer State Park while to the west the Hood Pond area forms a corridor of land running in a northwesterly direction to Georgetown-Rowley State Forest (Chapter 4) and tiny Cleaveland Farm State Forest. Most riders choose to explore either one side or the other.

Almost all of the trails are unnamed and unmarked. A few designated loops in the Pine Swamp Area have colored tree tags, and reference points have been added to the accompanying map to assist their description. The Pine Swamp Area has almost all easy riding, the Hood Pond Area has rougher conditions, and Bradley Palmer State Park has a combination of easy and intermediate trails.

Two marked loops provide an easy introduction to the Pine Swamp area's vast network of options. The **Red Trail**, designated by red tree tags, is a 5-mile easy cruise on carriage roads that encounters only a few small hills. Beginning at the footbridge trailhead on Topsfield Rd., the loop rises into the woods for a short distance, turns right at the first intersection, continues to the end and turns left (reference point **A** on the map). It stays straight for the next 1.2 miles and crosses a causeway through Willowdale Swamp along this distance. The Red Trail turns left at the next four-way intersection (reference point **B**) and then turns right a quarter-mile ahead, scrambling up a brief slope that is loose from erosion. Descending the other side of this hill, the loop turns left on a segment of the **Bay Circuit Trail**, skirts an open wetland, and emerges in a farm field under agricultural lease near Linebrook Rd. Here visitors are requested to remain on the trail and not disturb the crops. The Red Trail returns to the woods in a short distance heading westward along the ridgetop of an esker, then turns left (south) at the next major intersection (reference point **C**). Following the tree tags back to the trailhead, the loop bears right at the next two intersections and left at the third (reference point **D**), a half-mile from the starting point.

The similar, 4.5-mile **Blue Trail** is marked by blue tree tags, although it should be noted that many have faded in color and appear to be white. It overlaps much of the Red Trail but adds a more remote loop in an area of small hills near Pine Swamp Rd. and later short-cuts the area of fields near Linebrook Rd.

Riders looking for a longer tour can test their map reading skills on the maze of options in and around these routes. The less-traveled, grassy double-tracks typically make small side loops off the more heavily used trails. Riding the perimeter of the Pine Swamp Area's network is about an 8-mile trip, depending on the exact route taken.

Most of the Hood Pond area's double-tracks are rockier and hillier. The 1.7-mile **Esker Ridge Trail** heads northward from the parking area near Hood Pond, first with a quarter-mile of smooth riding and then with intermediate conditions over some moderate slopes and a steady stream of exposed rocks, which are avoidable. Most of the trail's course follows the crest of an esker, a ridgeline formed during the Ice Age by a sub-glacial stream.

Two intermediate-level trails intersect along this distance. One leaves the Esker Ridge Trail a half-mile from Boxford Rd. and runs eastward for a mile to Newbury Rd., while a second runs in the opposite direction to connect Cleaveland Farm State Forest.

Other double-tracks link Linebrook Rd. with Old Right Rd. over a distance of less than a mile. Lined by stone walls, these old farm roads are easy, level, and smooth.

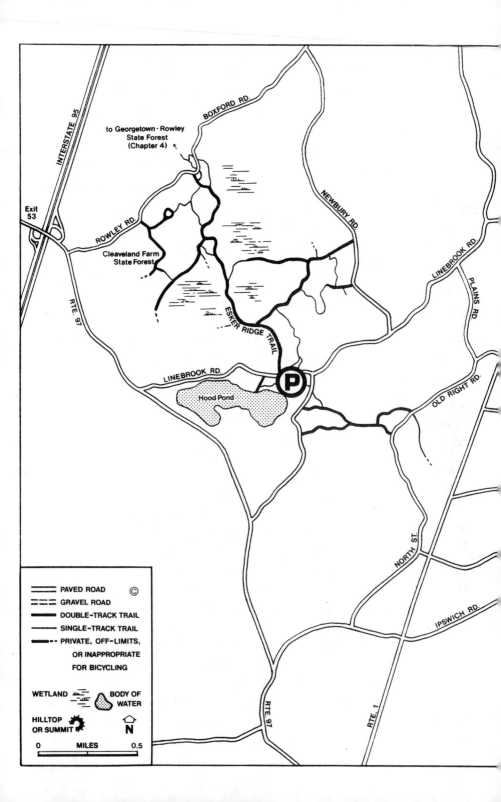

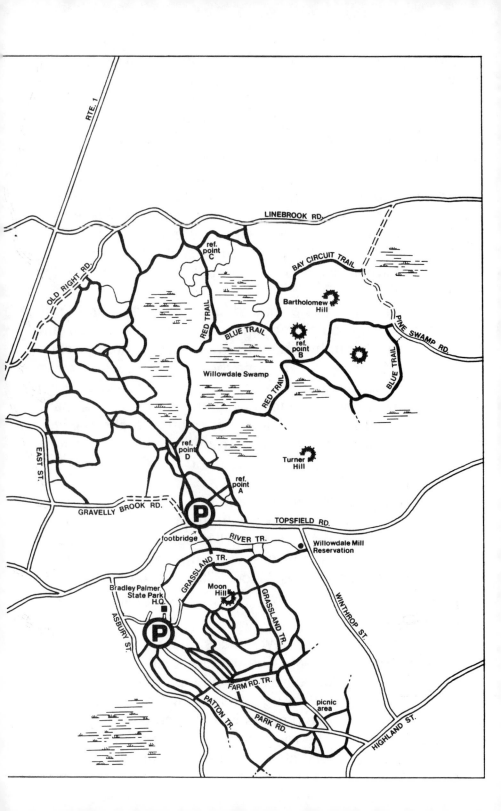

Use Old Right Rd. to cross Rte. 1 and provide the most direct linkage with the Pine Swamp Area.

Bradley Palmer State Park's tightly grouped trails can be confusing for newcomers but are worth a visit. The park's stone mansion, long fields, and river shoreline give it a distinctive atmosphere. Begin on the **Farm Road Trail** which leaves from the horse trailer parking area, not far from the headquarters complex. An easy dirt road, it starts beside a small pond and rises gradually into the woods with a smooth surface, enters a small clearing after 0.4 miles, and curves to the left at a 5-way intersection. It then enjoys a slight downhill slope for another 0.4 miles and ends at the edge of a field.

Turn left at this point and follow the **Grassland Trail**, a gently rolling route that connects a string of narrow hay fields running northward. The trail passes through short sections of woods that separate the fields but continues in a straight direction for a mile before turning westward. After heading westward for another half-mile, it ends at a metal gate where riders can continue straight on a short, paved road that returns to the trailhead near park headquarters. Combining the Farm Road Trail and the Grassland Trail makes an easy, 2.3-mile loop.

Two hills rise in the center of this loop to provide more strenuous alternatives with intermediate conditions. Trails ascend these slopes from all directions, some heading directly uphill and others winding on more gradual approaches. The top of Moon Hill has a broad field that allows a full view of the sky.

SINGLE-TRACKS:

Limited to only a few options, the area's single-track riding is short but sweet. The nameless path heading north from the parking lot near Hood Pond, paralleling the Esker Ridge Trail, is barely recognizable from the road amid the vines and foliage overgrowing its entrance and produces a challenging ride. The route encounters a series of difficult, small hills with eroded slopes that keep riders busy. To the east near Newbury Rd., a couple of smoother, flatter options wind through the woods for short distances.

The Pine Swamp Area has a cluster of single-tracks near its northern boundary that offer mostly intermediate conditions. Tight spaces, relatively smooth surfaces, and plenty of trees to dodge make them a fun ride.

The **River Trail** at Bradley Palmer State Park holds difficult riding and beautiful scenery along a mile of the Ipswich River. Guided by blue tree tags, it alternates between a narrow path that is rippled with tree roots and a wider, smoother surface that allows riders a chance to appreciate the water views.

DRIVING DIRECTIONS:

To park at Willowdale's Pine Swamp Area or Bradley Palmer State Park, take Exit 50 from I-95 and follow Rte. 1 north for 4 miles. Watch for signs for Bradley Palmer State Park and turn right on Ipswich Rd. at a traffic signal. To reach the park, continue east toward Ipswich for 1.2 miles, turn right on Asbury St., and then left at the park entrance. To reach the footbridge parking area, continue on Ipswich Rd. for another half-mile and park at the gravel turn-out.

To park at Hood Pond, take Exit 53 from I-95 and head south on Rte. 97 for 1 mile. Turn left on Linebrook Rd. and look for an unmarked, gravel turn-out 0.9 miles ahead on the right.

PUBLIC TRANSPORTATION:

The Rockport line runs to Ipswich. Turn left out of the station and follow Topsfield Rd. out of town for 3.5 miles, then look for trails on both sides of the road.

BIKE SHOPS:

Bay Road Bikes, 52 Railroad Ave., South Hamilton, Tel. (978) 468-1301

The Bicycle Shop, 17 Main St., Topsfield, Tel. (978) 887-6511

T & S Cycle, 67 Main St., Wenham, Tel. (978) 468-4488

Two for the Road, 74 E. Main St., Georgetown, Tel. (978) 352-7343

ADDITIONAL INFORMATION:

Willowdale State Forest, c/o Bradley Palmer State Park, Asbury St., Topsfield, MA 01983, Tel. (978) 887-5931

6
Bald Hill Reservation
Boxford

Old wagon roads make great recreational trails because they blend a sense of history with the natural surroundings. Miles of them await at Bald Hill and, together with the stone walls and a few cellar holes, speak to earlier times when the land was cleared and farming was the way of life. Today the rocks and roots on these well-worn roads make for intermediate and difficult mountain biking but a few routes hold smoother conditions.

BACKGROUND:

Bald Hill Reservation is a 1,624-acre collection of properties including state forest, state wildlife sanctuary, and private conservation land. The reservation originated in 1922 with a 120-acre donation by John Phillips for a wildlife preserve, then grew in the early 1960's when the Essex County Greenbelt Association fought plans for a 100-lot subdivision, leading the state to purchase the acreage. Later, a parcel of federal property used by the Department of Defense was transformed to state forest land. The area is managed in a coordinated effort by its various owners and a volunteer group, the Friends of Bald Hill, performs much of the trail maintenance.

TRAIL POLICIES:

Mountain bikers and equestrians are specifically requested not to ride at Bald Hill during mud season each year, typically in March and April, since the ground is especially vulnerable to erosion when it is soft. Certain trails within the reservation are always closed to bicycling and these are delineated on the map but not necessarily marked with signs. Remember that tire prints left on trails that are closed to mountain biking are a negative image in the minds of land managers and other trail users.

In addition, visitors should be careful not to stray onto abutting private lands since several trails leave the reservation. Swimming is not permitted and the area is closed one half hour after sunset. Signs posted at the Sharpner's Pond Rd. trailhead state that the parking lot gate is locked each day at 4:00 PM.

ORIENTATION:

Two trailheads provide starting points for a ride at Bald Hill. The Sharpner's Pond Rd. parking lot is easily accessible from Rte. 114 in North Andover while the Middleton Rd. lot is close to Interstate 95 and Boxford center.

A few trails are named but signs are not present to display them. Most intersections have a designated number that is posted on the trail and displayed on the map, making it easy to locate your position. This is fortunate since few natural features are present to provide other landmarks in this vast woodland.

DOUBLE-TRACKS:

Beginning at the Sharpner's Pond Rd. parking lot, one trail leads past the gate into the **Nike Site**, a large clearing which was to be developed by the U.S. Department of Defense as an anti-ballistic missile radar site. Although the project was never completed, 23 acres remain stripped of topsoil and a deep hole blasted through bedrock, now filled with water, marks the planned location of a radar tower. A barren expanse of gravel and scrub trees at the Nike Site creates a distinctive atmosphere.

The easy, 1.5-mile **Fuller Loop** extends northward from this area with the welcome shade of pine forest. The route links intersections 3, 4, and 5 with generally smooth conditions and a few brief hills.

The bumpy **Bald Hill Trail** leaves the Nike Site at intersection 2 on a 2-mile course to the base of 247-foot **Bald Hill**, one of the reservation's most popular landmarks. A hayfield on top of the hill allows a view once the leaves

50

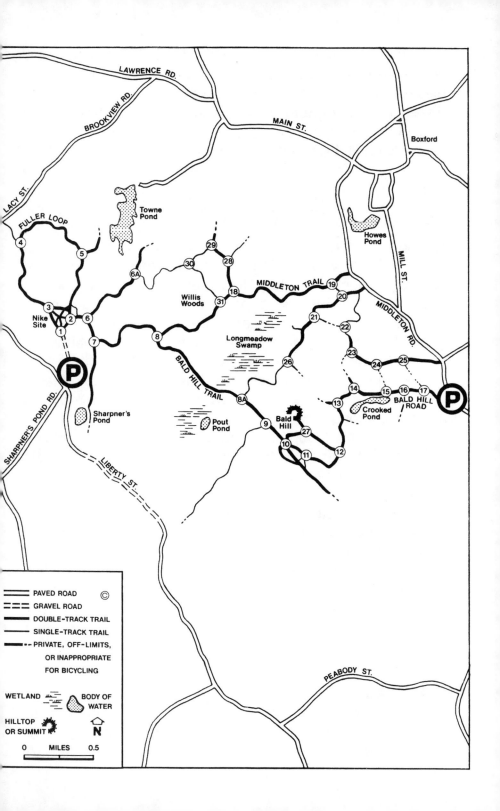

have fallen. An old wagon road, Bald Hill Trail is now rippled with a steady supply of rocks and roots. It rolls over small hills near intersection 8, drops to a stream bed feeding **Pout Pond**, and rises gradually for the last half-mile to the foot of Bald Hill.

Bald Hill Road allows an easier approach to Bald Hill from the Middleton Rd. trailhead. Passing along the northern shoreline of scenic **Crooked Pond**, the road crosses an inlet brook and begins to climb the base of the hill at the 1-mile mark. Erosion has left a rocky surface in a few spots but the road becomes smoother as it levels near intersection 12 and circles to the south side of the hill where several meadows unfold. Near intersection 10 an obscure sign marks the Russell-Hooper homesite, once a farm of 50 acres and now merely a cellarhole.

Running along the reservation's northern boundary, the **Middleton Trail** is grassy and smooth except for a scattering of avoidable rocks that bulge through its surface. It encounters no major elevation changes as it gently rolls and turns through the woods.

A 6.6-mile loop starts from the Sharpner's Pond Rd. trailhead with mostly intermediate riding and a few spots with difficult conditions. Turn right at intersections 1, 2, and 6 and then left at intersection 7 to follow the Bald Hill Trail east. At intersection 8 turn left and take the Middleton Trail to its endpoint on Middleton Rd., then turn right and follow the pavement for 0.9 miles to the parking turnout, metal gate, and trailhead map at the end of Bald Hill Road. Follow Bald Hill Road to the south slope of Bald Hill and at the far end of the meadows find the Bald Hill Trail starting from intersection 10. Continue straight on the Bald Hill Trail past intersection 8 and retrace your course past intersections 7, 6, 2, and 1 back to the Nike Site.

SINGLE-TRACKS:

Most of the reservation's single-tracks are closed to mountain biking but there are a few fragments open to riding. The trail running between intersections 20 and 8A

52

above **Longmeadow Swamp** starts as a fairly restful double-track and then changes to a difficult single-track with rocks and roots breaking the surface. Across the wetland, look for two narrow paths spanning the distance between intersections 6A and 31 with intermediate conditions in the area of **Willis Woods**.

DRIVING DIRECTIONS:

From I-495 take Exit 42A and follow Rte. 114 east for 6 miles. Turn left on Sharpner's Pond Rd. and drive for 1.7 miles to the parking lot at the end.

From I-95 take Exit 47B and follow Rte. 114 west for 6 miles. Turn right on Sharpner's Pond Rd., just past the North Andover town line, and park at the end.

To reach the Middleton Rd. trailhead in Boxford, take Exit 51 from I-95 and follow Endicott St. west toward Middleton. Turn immediately right on Middleton Rd. and find the trailhead sign and small parking area 1.5 miles ahead on the left.

BIKE SHOPS:

Bay Road Bikes, 18 Bay Road, Hamilton, Tel. (978) 468-1301

Cycle Stop, 26 Chestnut St., Andover, Tel. (978) 975-1515

Eastern Cycle, 59 Main St., North Andover, Tel. (978) 686-0211

Landry's Cycling, 151 Endicott St., Danvers, Tel. (978) 777-3337

Pro Cycles, 20A Main St. (Rte. 28), North Reading, Tel. (978) 664-9762

Ski Market, Endicott Plaza, Danvers, (978) 777-3344

T&S Cycle, 67 Main St., Wenham, Tel. (978) 468-4488

The Bicycle Shop, 17 Main St., Topsfield, Tel. (978) 887-6511

Two for the Road, 74 E. Main St. (Rte. 133), Georgetown, Tel. (978) 352-7343

Western Cycle, 22 Maple St.(Rte. 62), Danvers, Tel. (978) 774-1685

ADDITIONAL INFORMATION:

Boxford State Forest, c/o Harold Parker State Forest, 1951 Turnpike Rd., North Andover, MA 01845, Tel. (978) 686-3391

Essex County Greenbelt Association, 82 Eastern Ave., Essex, MA 01929, Tel. (978) 768-7241

J.C. Phillips Wildlife Sanctuary, Massachusetts Department of Fisheries and Wildlife, P.O. Box 86, Acton, MA 01720, Tel. (978) 263-4347

7
Harold Parker State Forest
North Andover

Harold Parker's 30 or so miles of trails spread across 3,100 acres of woodland and water views. The core of its mountain biking trail network is a set of easy and intermediate double-tracks that is suitable for a first-ever ride or an easy cruise, while a growing number of tight single-tracks keeps expert riders happy too.

BACKGROUND:

Originating in 1916, this property is the second oldest state forest in Massachusetts and is named in honor of an early highway engineer who was a leader in establishing a system of public lands. Harold Parker served as chairman of the Massachusetts State Forest Commission and laid the groundwork for the acquisition of public lands throughout the state. Totaling over 270,000 acres, these properties now comprise one of the country's largest forest and park systems.

Today, the vast area of Harold Parker State Forest attracts many interests. Fishermen line the banks of its numerous ponds, swimmers enjoy a beautiful new beach area, horseback riders venture from surrounding farms, and campers have the opportunity to spend the night. Along with mountain bikers and hikers traveling its trails, the forest's visitors coexist remarkably well.

TRAIL POLICIES:

No restrictions currently exist on mountain biking at Harold Parker and all trails are open for riding. The Forest Supervisor is quick to warn, however, that the multi-use policy will remain only if cyclists abide by the area's rules and are not a burden to the environment or to other visitors. Snowmobilers and other motorized visitors once had the chance to use these trails but are now excluded because they abused the privilege. Please do your part to see that bicycles remain welcome.

Mountain bikers are requested to stay on designated trails, ride in control at all times, and avoid startling hikers and horseback riders by announcing your presence at a safe distance. As with any area, it is not acceptable to ride when the ground is wet since the soil is soft and vulnerable to erosion. All visitors should note that parts of this state forest are open for hunting at certain times of the year.

ORIENTATION:

Wooden signs display the names of a few trails but plan to depend on the trail map to find your way through this large area. Public roads that pass through the forest and numerous ponds can be helpful in plotting your location but few other noticeable landmarks exist.

Four off-street trailhead parking areas are located in various parts of the property but many smaller spots also exist. The **Forest Headquarters** lot serves the gravel roads and double-track trails in the eastern area while the **Collins Pond** lot accesses the easy double-tracks and great single-tracks in the west. In the center are parking lots on both ends of **Berry Pond Road**, although the one at the northern end is intended for beach access in summer, when a small fee is charged. This lot also offers public toilets.

GRAVEL ROADS:

The several miles of gated, gravel roads surrounding Forest Headquarters on Middleton Rd. were built by the Civilian Conservation Corps during the Great Depression. Among the easiest to pedal, **Stearns Pond Road** has a firm surface and pretty water views along its relatively flat course of 1.5 miles. To find it from the trailhead, pass through the brown metal gate at the end of the parking lot and follow the pavement of **Beach Road** to the end, then turn left.

Across the street from headquarters, **Harold Parker Road** leaves on an easy, mile-long route to the parking lot at the southern end of Berry Pond Road. With the exception of one hill where erosion has loosened the surface, the riding is trouble-free.

Bradford Pond Road starts on the left, a quarter-mile from headquarters. It forks southward to traverse some of the forest's biggest hills and ends after 1.5 miles at Marblehead St. Watch for loose stones on the slopes of this road making the ups more difficult and the downs a bit tricky. **Salem Pond Road** and **Upper Salem Pond Road**, both less than a mile in length, return to Middleton Rd. with similar conditions and pass the ponds bearing the same names. Combining Harold Parker Road, Bradford Pond Road, Salem Pond Road, and Middleton Rd. creates a 2.5-mile loop from headquarters.

DOUBLE-TRACKS:

Easy and intermediate-level mountain biking awaits on the forest's double-track trails. To the southeast of headquarters, Upper **Sudden Pond Road** takes an easy route past **Sudden Pond** to the property boundary and intersects two rockier double-tracks along the way. One runs southward to a scenic picnic area overlooking the water.

Alone to the north in some of Harold Parker's most remote reaches, **Pine Road** and **Boulder Road** combine to form 0.8 miles of flat riding on grassy double-track. Absent of the ponds and natural attractions of other portions of the forest, this area gets little use and its small collection of trails is typically abandoned. Outside of this loop are three unnamed double-tracks that explore much more territory but require intermediate riding skills as they encounter small hills, rocky surfaces, and a few wet spots. These outer trails are linked by single-tracks that form part of the **Bay Circuit**, a partially completed trail which will circle the Boston area from Plum Island to Duxbury.

A pretty array of ponds marks the western bounds with plenty of soothing scenery. These ponds were created during the Great Depression by the Civilian Conservation Corps, which also planted many of the trees and built most

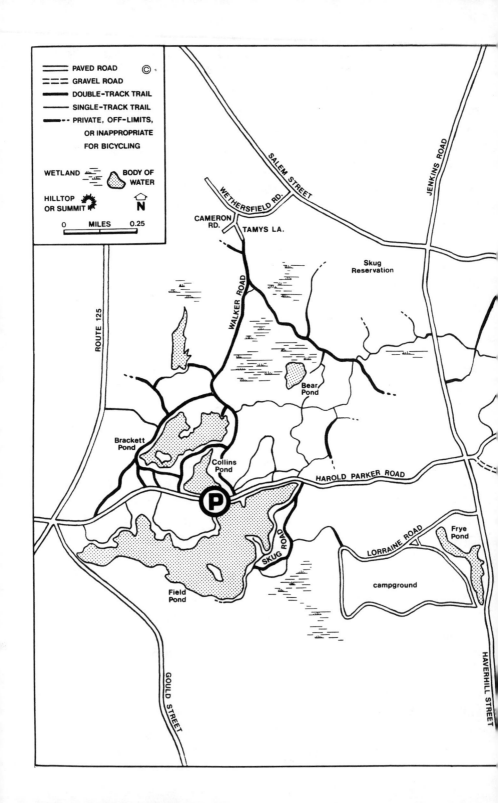

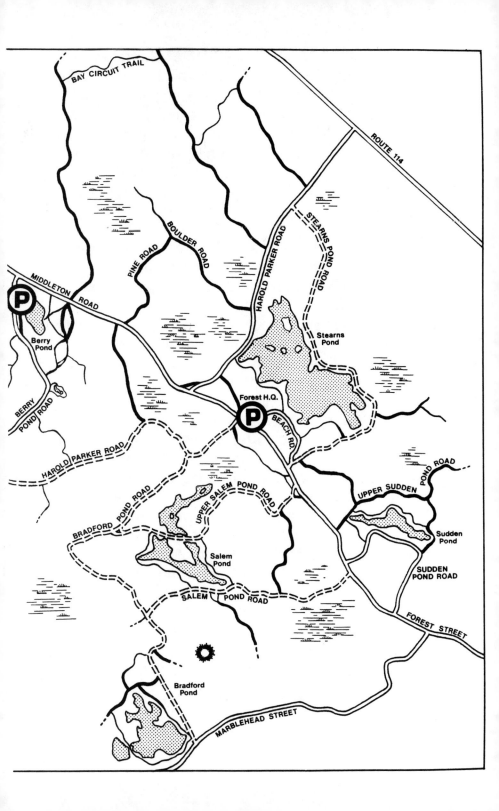

of the roads in the area. Shady **Walker Road** heads north along the eastern shores of Collins and Brackett ponds on its way to the end of Tamys La. with only a few roots and rocks to avoid. Two other double-tracks intersect on the left to circle the ponds with generally easy riding and more nice views. Across the pavement, **Skug Road** ventures south for a half-mile along the flat shoreline of **Field Pond**, the forest's largest body of water and one of its most popular with fishermen.

SINGLE-TRACKS:

The many nameless single-track trails have generally intermediate and difficult conditions for mountain biking and are mostly found in the western half of the forest. Two smooth loops bounce along the northern shoreline of Field Pond past secret fishing spots while a larger area of single-tracks south of **Bear Pond** tackles hillier terrain. This cluster of paths is especially recommended for its rideable hills, many turns, and tight spaces.

It is possible to continue eastward on single-track to Jenkins Rd. where another group of narrow paths unfolds near **Berry Pond**. Known for its swimming beach, toilet facilities, and picnic pavilion, the Berry Pond area and surrounding trails can be busy during the summer so ride accordingly. Single-tracks spread in all directions with challenging routes on both sides of Berry Pond Road.

Other brief but enjoyable segments lie along the shoreline of **Salem Pond**. The path along the eastern side explores rocky terrain while the one along the western side, knee-deep in blueberry bushes, is a smoother ride except for a stairway of rocks at one point. The 0.5-mile path along Sudden Pond's northern bank is wrinkled with small hills and tight turns and makes a worthy adventure.

DRIVING DIRECTIONS:

From I-93 take Exit 41 and follow Rte. 125 north for 2.5 miles to a state police barricks on the right. Turn right on Harold Parker Rd. and the parking lot at Collins Pond is just ahead. To reach the Forest Headquarters lot continue for another mile to Jenkins Rd., turn left and drive for 0.8 miles, then turn right on Middleton Rd. The parking lot is 1.2 miles ahead on the left.

From I-495 take Exit 42A and follow Rte. 114 east for 5.5 miles. Turn right on Harold Parker Rd. and drive for 1 mile to the end, turn left on Middleton Rd. and the Forest Headquarters lot is ahead on the left.

BIKE SHOPS:

The Bicycle Shop, 17 Main St., Topsfield, Tel. (978) 887-6511

Cycle Stop, 26 Chestnut St., Andover, Tel. (978) 975-1515

Eastern Cycle, 59 Main St., North Andover, Tel. (978) 686-0211

Pro Cycles, 20A Main St. (Rte. 28), North Reading, Tel. (978) 664-9762

ADDITIONAL INFORMATION:

Harold Parker State Forest, 1951 Turnpike Rd., North Andover, MA 01845-6326, Tel. (978) 686-3391

Bay Circuit Alliance, 3 Railroad St., Andover, MA 01810

8
Lynn Woods Reservation
Lynn

Lynn Woods is a treasure of trails where few would think to look. Surrounded by civilization and only 10 miles north of Boston, these 2,200 acres comprise the second largest municipal park in the United States and one of the most popular places to mountain bike in Massachusetts. The vast number of trails provides a ride for every ability.

BACKGROUND:

Lynn Woods was purchased from native inhabitants in 1687. Its rocky hills were originally used as common land for grazing livestock and cutting wood, and efforts to preserve the land in perpetuity date from 1881 under the leadership of Cyrus Tracy, a local naturalist who saw the long-term value of its wilderness. In addition to a great trail resource, the property serves as a water supply for the city.

The reservation has attracted unwanted activities over the years, including the disposal of stolen cars and the setting of brush fires, and policing the huge area has proven to be a challenge. Happily, the regular flow of mountain bikers and others along the roads and trails is viewed as a helpful deterent to this mischief but the visual effects sadden the scenery at a few locations.

Two volunteer groups, the Friends of Lynn Woods and the New England Mountain Bike Association (NEMBA), have made great efforts in maintaining the reservation's trails by repairing eroded hills and constructing boardwalks at wet areas. Plenty of more work remains to be done and volunteers interested in joining the cause are urged to contact NEMBA or the Friends of Lynn Woods.

TRAIL POLICIES:

Mountain bikers have earned a welcome place on the trails of Lynn Woods and it is important that it be preserved.

Biking is permitted from April 16 through December 31 each year and prohibited from January 1 through April 15 in order to minimize damage to trail surfaces. In addition, bicycles are only welcome on gravel roads, white-blazed trails, and blue-blazed trails. Riding on any other trail is prohibited.

Be aware that the roads and trails in Lynn Woods get heavy use on weekends from a variety of activities and that bicyclists are expected to yield to hikers and horseback riders at all times. Some gravel roads have sizeable downhill slopes so it is important that mountain bikers remain at safe speeds, keep to the right, and be ready to yield. Swimming in the ponds is not allowed and the area officially closes at sunset each day.

ORIENTATION:

The trail network at Lynn Woods is vast but finding your way with a map is made easier by several features. Wooden, routed signs are posted on trees to display the names of the main roads and trails, and numbered signs (displayed on the map) are posted on trees at major intersections. Note that these numbered signs are very small and can be difficult to notice. Only the trails that are open to mountain biking appear on the accompanying map.

The trails are divided into two parts by the long shape of Walden Pond with trailhead parking lots serving each side. The area south of the pond holds a full range of routes ranging from easy gravel roads to difficult single-track, while the area north of the pond is concentrated with intermediate and difficult single- and double-tracks.

GRAVEL ROADS:

The extensive network of graded, gravel roads is suited for easy touring but some routes encounter big hills with loose surfaces. If you cannot ride up these slopes, it could be worth walking your bike up them because these roads lead to some of the reservation's best views including distant vistas of the ocean and Boston skyline.

Pennybrook Road is among the flattest to ride and

heads north from the western gate for a mile toward Walden Pond. It turns through the woods between Tomlins Swamp and the base of Mt. Moriah until it reaches Intersection C5-5 where **Walden Pond Road** forks left along the pond and **Great Woods Road** veers right on a course to eastern gate. Great Woods Road rolls for 2 miles along the shore of the pond with a few small hills and pretty views over the water.

Dungeon Road is a 1.4-mile ride over several hills to one of the reservation's most intriguing historical sites, Dungeon Rock, where a 135-foot-deep cave is said to be the final resting place of a pirate and his treasure, trapped and sealed by rock in an earthquake in 1658. The cave's present entrance and long passageway were blasted in the 1800's in a fruitless effort to find the treasure. Near Breed's Pond, Dungeon Road joins **Waycross Road** which returns to Pennybrook Road near western gate. Combining Pennybrook Road, Great Woods Road, Dungeon Road, and Waycross Road is a 4.3-mile loop from the western gate.

Two other roads offer diversions to nearby hilltops with great views. **Loop Road** starts at the intersection of Great Woods and Dungeon roads (D5-7), climbs to the top of Mt. Gilead where a stunning view of Boston awaits, and then descends back to Dungeon Road. **Cooke Road** climbs neighboring 285-foot Burrill Hill and offers another great view from a stone tower built during the Great Depression. Bicyclists should watch their speeds when descending these hills since the road surfaces have loose rocks.

DOUBLE-TRACKS:

Many of the surrounding double-track trails are made tricky by rocky slopes, but interlying flat sections are often smooth and relatively easy. This is the case with the **Jackson Path** which leaves the western gate with easy rolling to Breed's Pond, then climbs over a short but steep hill that is braced with water bars to prevent erosion. Similarly, the double-tracks south and west of Pennybrook Road have alternating sections of intermediate and difficult riding in a landscape of rocky knolls and woodlands.

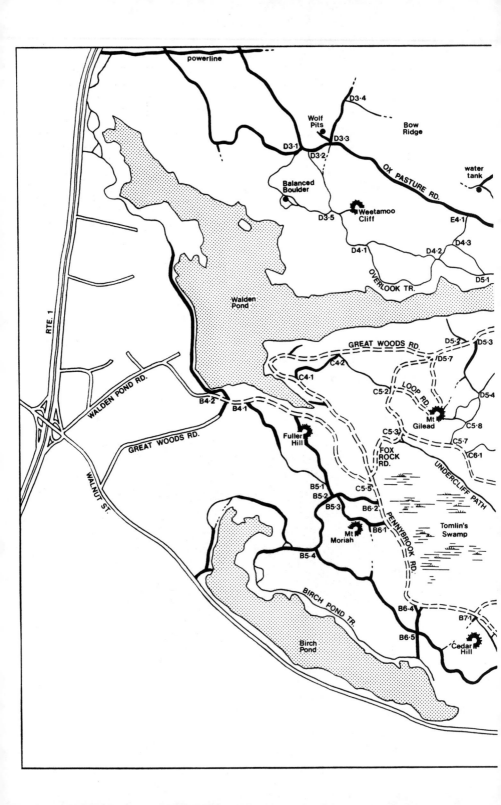

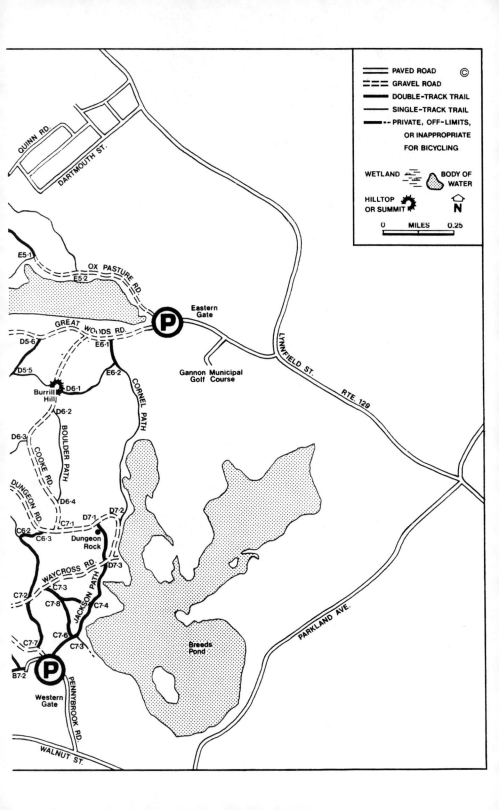

North of Walden Pond, **Ox Pasture Road** leads mountain bikers from the eastern gate trailhead to an area of challenging hills. One of Lynn Woods' oldest, this wagon road explores an area of low hills and rock outcroppings, rising for most of its 2-mile length toward Rte.1 at the reservation's northern boundary. Veering right from the parking lot, the road starts with a gravel surface and a short climb, crosses a shelf cut into a slope above the pond, then descends back to the shoreline where it loses the gravel surface. Ox Pasture Road narrows at this point and becomes a bumpier ride over rocks and ruts, especially on the slopes, but these obstacles are either avoidable or short-lived so the riding is generally intermediate.

Near intersection D3-3, approximately 1.5 miles from the parking lot, Ox Pasture Road passes the Wolf Pits, peculiar relics of early colonial times. Wolves were a constant threat to settlers in the 1600's and these pits, 8 feet deep and lined with stone, formed an effective means of capturing them. The holes were covered with pine boughs, baited with rabbits, and too deep for the wolves to escape.

SINGLE-TRACKS:

Most of Lynn's single-tracks are rated as difficult for mountain biking since an abundance of rocks and hills await along their courses. A popular collection branches from the **Overlook Trail** north of Walden Pond where tight paths mold themselves to an abrupt and unique terrain of granite knolls and huge boulders. The Overlook Trail starts at E5-1 on Ox Pasture Road and threads along the shore of the pond with several steep ups and downs, passing great views over the water at high points along the way.

It is possible to ride around the western end of Walden Pond using a single-track that parallels Rte. 1, but the rocks and narrow spaces of this 1.5-mile path make it a technical ride. Lots of tire tracks attest to its popularity.

South of Walden Pond, good single-tracks await in the area near Mt. Gilead and Burrill Hill. **Boulder Path** and the other trails that reach the summits are most rideable in their downhill directions and encounter challenging collections of rocks, water bars, and steep drops.

The mile-long **Undercliff Path** follows a difficult shelf of land between ledges at the base of Mt. Gilead and the edge of Tomlin's Swamp. Beginning on Waycross Road as an easy double-track, the trail deteriorates to a rough footpath with piles of rocks and a few wet spots.

Milder conditions exist on the white-blazed **Cornel Path** which enjoys a smooth, earthen surface for part of its 0.7-mile length. Avoidable rocks and some newly-placed waterbars make the rest of it intermediate riding. The trail connects Great Woods Road near eastern gate with Dungeon Road and borders the Gannon Municipal Golf Course near the midpoint, where trail users are requested to show proper courtesy by being as quiet as possible.

Avoid the **Birch Pond Trail** which runs along the northern shore of Birch Pond. Although the trail is blazed in white and open to biking, it is a boneyard of rocks and offers few places for tires to roll easily.

DRIVING DIRECTIONS:

To reach the western entrance from Rte. 128, take Exit 44A for Rte. 1 south. Take the Walnut St. exit, drive for 2.1 miles toward Lynn, then turn left on Pennybrook Rd. Park at the end.

To reach the eastern entrance from Rte. 128, take Exit 44B and follow signs for Rte. 129 east. After 2 miles, turn right on Great Woods Rd. and continue straight ahead to the parking lot.

BIKE SHOPS:

Lynn Shore Cycles, 251 Western Ave., Lynn, Tel. (781) 581-2700

Northeast Bicycles, 102 Broadway (Rte. 1), Saugus, Tel. (781) 233-2664

ADDITIONAL INFORMATION:

The Friends of Lynn Woods, P.O. Box 8216, Lynn, MA 01904, www.flw.org, Tel. (781) 593-7773

Lynn Parks Department, Lynn City Hall, Lynn, MA 01904, Tel. (781) 598–4000

NEMBA, P.O. Box 2221, Acton, MA 01720-2221, www.nemba.org, Tel. (800) 57-NEMBA

9
Middlesex Fells Reservation
Stoneham

One of Boston's favorite mountain biking areas, the Fells is a 2,000-acre preserve located only a few miles north of the city with plenty of trails to explore. Single-track riding is limited but conditions on the double-tracks range from easy to difficult and include lots of hills, some with views.

BACKGROUND:

Fells is an English word for rocky, windblown hills and it is a fitting name. If it were not for the bustle of nearby civilization and the dull roar of Interstate 93, the reservation's open ledges and viewpoints might seem like real mountain tops. This rough terrain spared the property from much settlement in colonial times and in 1894 it was formally established as a parkland, part of the so-called *emerald necklace* of open space that surrounds Boston.

TRAIL POLICIES:

The Metropolitan District Commission (MDC) manages the Middlesex Fells Reservation and has a specific policy regarding mountain biking. It permits bicycles on all double-tracks (trails that are wide enough to accommodate a four-wheeled vehicle) and on a few sections of designated single-track that are marked as being open to biking. The many remaining miles of single-track paths are strictly off-limits and are usually posted with small, white signs bearing the *No Bikes* symbol. Since many of these paths were designed for hiking their steep slopes have proven to be incapable of sustaining other uses.

Mountain biking is not permitted anywhere in the reservation between January 1 and April 15 each year when trail surfaces can be vulnerable to ruts and erosion. The areas immediately surrounding several water reservoirs are posted as being closed to the public. High traffic levels at the Fells, especially on weekends, make responsible riding habits a priority so keep to a safe speed, be ready to yield trail, and never ride when the ground is wet. Since policies could change, check trailhead notice boards before you ride.

The New England Mountain Bike Association (NEMBA) has made great progress at insuring a future for mountain biking in the reservation but this work is never done. The organization performs an annual series of trail maintenance projects, sponsors a trail patrol program, schedules group rides, and continues to work toward gaining bicycle access to more single-tracks. To this end, NEMBA urges riders to protect their place in the trail community by adhering to the reservation's policies and by volunteering for the trail work projects whenever possible.

ORIENTATION:

I-93 and several local roads divide the reservation and provide a useful means of orientation for visitors. The primary parking lots shown on the map serve each area but smaller spaces access many additional trailheads.

Numbers posted on the gates that block vehicle access at trail/road intersections allow another means of determining location since these numbers are displayed on the accompanying map. Note that many trails are named but not all are marked by signs, so first-time visitors should bring a map and carefully track their courses.

DOUBLE-TRACKS:

The Sheepfold trailhead is a popular one with cyclists and the most central starting point for a ride, but the parking lot is often full on weekends. A flat, easy ride extends northward on the **abandoned railroad bed** that parallels the Fellsway West for almost a mile. Continuing north, look for 0.8-mile **Bear Hill Road** forking to the left with a broad surface as it climbs to the top of 317' Bear Hill where a viewing tower offers a 360-degree vista.

Easy options south of Sheepfold include **Brooks Road** and **Silver Mine Path** which link to form a rolling, mile-long cruise. They are noisy from the highway at a few points but deliver riders to the **Bellevue Pond Loop**, a quieter, 2.7-mile circuit originating at the Bellevue Pond trailhead with more rolling hills and occasional rocks on the surface. At Bellevue look for the gravel road ascending nearby 243' Pine Hill where another tower allows a bird's eye view of Boston. The steady, uphill grind is sure to bring a rise in any pedaler's heart rate but ride cautiously on the return descent since this is a favorite place for walkers.

Lawrence Woods is a forgotten corner of mellow hills and grassy double-tracks located south of Border Rd. A haven for easy mountain biking, this area gets little use so trails like **Rams Head Road** and the **Whitmore Brook Road** have a deserted feel. Riding the perimeter of this network of trails creates a 2.4-mile loop off the pavement.

The Long Pond Trailhead serves the area west of the three Winchester reservoirs where more hill climbs and deep forest scenery await. **West Dam Path** and **Molly's Spring Road** are both smooth and level as they approach South Reservoir but the trail linking the two has a sizeable climb and descent. Be sure to try the **Cranberry Pool Path** which passes beautiful Long Pond, a slender pool lined with ledge and overhanging trees.

A 6.2-mile marked mountain biking loop circling the three Winchester reservoirs is described in detail in the *Single-Track* portion of this chapter.

Heading east, it is possible to reach many more miles of fire roads by passing beneath I-93 on the Fellsway West and following trails south of Spot Pond. Look for the shoreline **Pickerel Path** leaving from gate 28 or the smoother, flatter **Half Mile Road** leaving from gate 29 to connect with Woodland Rd.

Others may choose to park at the roadside lot on Wyoming Ave. near Reservation Headquarters. A ride on the trail through Virginia Wood, once the site of several mills, is a peaceful affair in tranquil forest and forms the first leg of a 3.5-mile ride. Cross Ravine Rd. and continue southward

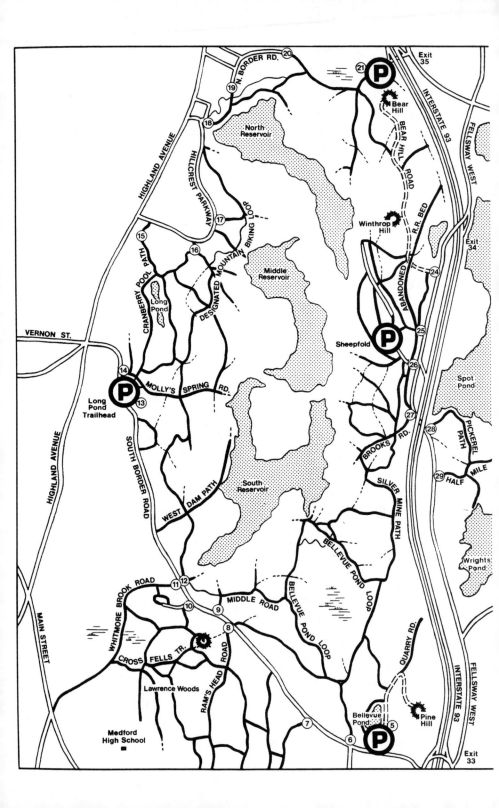

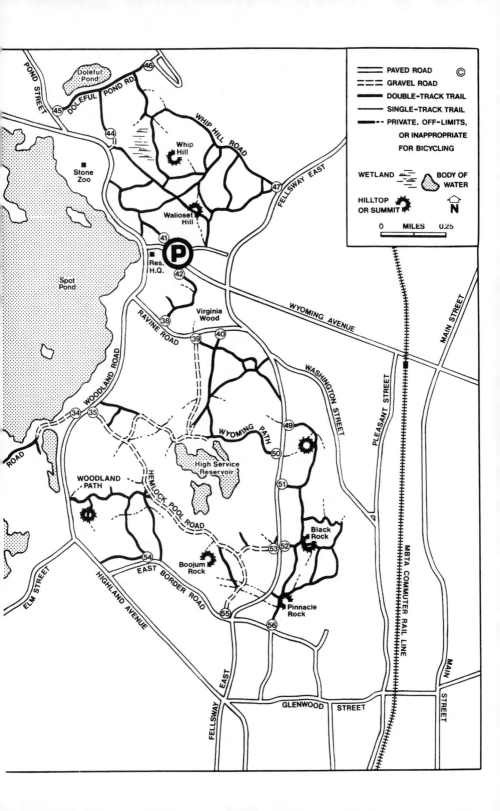

PAVED ROAD ©
GRAVEL ROAD
DOUBLE-TRACK TRAIL
SINGLE-TRACK TRAIL
PRIVATE, OFF-LIMITS,
OR INAPPROPRIATE
FOR BICYCLING

WETLAND   BODY OF
            WATER
HILLTOP
OR SUMMIT   N

0   MILES   0.25

POND STREET

Doleful
Pond

45
DOLEFUL POND RD.
46

44

WHIP HILL ROAD

Whip
Hill

47
FELLSWAY EAST

Stone
Zoo

Walioset
Hill

41
P
Res.
H.Q.
42

Spot
Pond

38
RAVINE ROAD
Virginia
Wood

39   40

WYOMING AVENUE

WOODLAND ROAD

MAIN STREET

34 35

WYOMING PATH

WASHINGTON STREET

49
50

High Service
Reservoir

51

WOODLAND
PATH

HEMLOCK POOL ROAD

PLEASANT STREET

Black
Rock

53 52

54
EAST BORDER ROAD

Boojum
Rock

MBTA COMMUTER RAIL LINE

ELM STREET

HIGHLAND AVENUE

55

56
Pinnacle
Rock

FELLSWAY EAST

GLENWOOD   STREET

MAIN STREET

on a gravel road that climbs a long, straight hill to a chainlink fence surrounding the High Service Reservoir. Turn right at this high point and descend to Woodland Rd., then turn left to reach **Hemlock Pool Road** which rises gradually from gate 35 amid rocky knobs and oak forest. It crests a hill after a half-mile and coasts down the opposite side, forking left before reaching the Fellsway East at gate 53. Returning to Virginia Wood by road is a 1.5-mile ride.

The Fells' most difficult double-tracks lie between Fellsway East and Washington St. The fire roads in this area tackle some of the roughest terrain, scrambling through passes between hills and reaching numerous elevations with excellent views. Black Rock and Pinnacle Rock are both inspiring spots to take a break. Beware of the loose rocks that litter the surface of these trails in places, especially in fall when they are obscured by leaves.

The slopes of Walioset Hill affect many trails north of Wyoming Ave. To avoid them, take the Fellsway East to **Whip Hill Road**, an old wagon track following the reservation's northern boundary to Whip Hill. Visiting the tall marsh grasses at nearby Doleful Pond make **Doleful Pond Road** a scenic extension to this ride. Linking the trails at the perimeter of this area (excluding Doleful Pond Road) creates an intermediate, 2-mile loop.

SINGLE-TRACKS:

The Fells' single-track riding is both extremely limited and very popular. Ranging from intermediate to difficult, sections of single-track are aligned around the three Winchester Reservoirs and, together with fire roads, form a marked, 6.2-mile **Designated Mountain Biking Loop**. Cyclists can take this loop in either direction and should expect to encounter many other pedalers on fairweather weekend days.

Following the loop in the clockwise direction from Sheepfold, riders head south on fire roads watching for the square, red tree tags labeled *Mountain Bike Loop* that mark the course. The first piece of single-track, a short, twisted

76

trail that wraps through an area of ledge and rocks, appears after a mile near the Bellevue Pond Loop. The route then turns westward on **Middle Road** before rising and falling on a second single-track that is ribbed with tree roots and water bars in the area between gates 9 and 12.

Heading northward, the loop remains on fire roads for the next 1.5 miles and then turns right on a segment of the Reservoir Trail, a difficult single-track with obstacles ranging from exposed rocks and roots to bridges and water bars. After descending beside the pavement of Hillcrest Pkwy., look for a small brick garage beside the water on the right. The trail drops into woods beside this building and turns in switchbacks on the slopes of hills near North Border Rd. before circling southward and finishing on double-track.

DRIVING DIRECTIONS:

The reservation is bisected by I-93 and accessed by exits 33, 34, and 35 as shown on the trail map. Note that Exit 35 serves only traffic to and from the north and Exit 34 serves only traffic to and from the south.

PUBLIC TRANSPORTATION:

The Lowell commuter rail line stops at Winchester center. From the station, follow Waterfield Rd. east to Mystic Valley Pkwy. Turn left and continue up the hill to the second traffic signal, then turn right on S. Border Rd. Look for trails on the left.

The Haverhill/Reading line stops at two points in Melrose. From the Wyoming Hill station, follow Wyoming Ave. west for 1 mile and look for trails on both sides of the road.

BIKE SHOPS:

City Cycle, 286 Main St., Stoneham, Tel. (781) 438-0358
Pro Cycles, 521 Main St., Melrose, Tel. (781) 662-2813
Wakefield Schwinn Cyclery, 16 Albion St., Wakefield, Tel. (781) 245-2342

ADDITIONAL INFORMATION:

Middlesex Fells Reservation, 1 Woodland Rd., Stoneham, MA 02180, Tel. (781) 662-5214
New England Mountain Bike Association, Tel. (800) 57-NEMBA , www.nemba. org

10
Great Brook Farm State Park
Carlisle

Great Brook is many places all in one: a busy park, a working farm, an ice cream stand, a cross country ski area, and a popular place for mountain biking. The riding includes both easy woods roads and challenging single-tracks.

BACKGROUND:

This 950-acre park was purchased by the state in 1974, in part to preserve a bit of New England's farming heritage. The dairy farm operates under a lease agreement and offers an interpretive program that allows the public to see and learn about farming practices. Barn tours are scheduled by the park staff during the warm season.

Great Brook Farm State Park attracts hundreds of visitors on weekends so be prepared to share the trails. Fortunately for mountain bikers, numerous New England Mountain Bike Association (NEMBA) trail maintenance projects have made a positive impression at the park and on its staff. These projects include the construction of bridges and boardwalks over wet areas, placement of water bars on eroding slopes, rerouting of segments of trail to more sustainable places, and construction of new single-tracks. Since this work is never done, NEMBA invites you to join in the fun and volunteer for a trail maintenance day.

TRAIL POLICIES:

The park supervisor cautions that cyclists should tread lightly as high traffic levels and erosion of trail surfaces are testing the limits of many routes. Ride at a safe speed, yield to hikers and equestrians, and never ride when the ground is wet.

Visitors are requested to be respectful of the farm operation by not disturbing the animals and by remaining at the edges of fields to avoid damaging crops. Signs around the farm complex, which includes a residence, designate the area as being off-limits to the general public.

In addition, most trails east of Lowell St. are groomed for cross country skiing during the winter months. When adequate snow cover exists between mid-December and mid-March these trails are open only to paid cross country skiers, and the staff at the ski touring center ask that you use the trails west of Lowell St. during these periods.

ORIENTATION:

Many of the trails are named and marked with wooden, routed signs and/or blue, plastic tree tags that display a symbol for the trail's name. Intersection numbers are posted at various points along the trails and are shown on the map to help visitors identify their location.

The park is divided into four sections by the pavement of Lowell St., North Rd., and Curve St. The busiest trails are east of Lowell St. and include easy double-tracks that circle scenic farmland, ponds, and woods, while less-traveled single-tracks await west of Lowell St.

DOUBLE-TRACKS:

Two large parking lots provide starting points at the center of the park. Easy riding begins at both with the 1-mile **Lantern Loop** and 1.1-mile **Litchfield Loop** offering smooth, open surfaces along the edges of open fields.

The park's most popular trail is the **Pine Point Loop**, an easy, 1.6-mile course circling Meadow Pond with the varied scenery of deep forests, fields, and wetlands. Hills are small and the trail surface is smooth except where the roots of surrounding white pines are exposed. From the parking lot near the farm, the Pine Point Loop starts across North Rd. in an area of mowed grass known as the meadows and follows a gravel road across a stone bridge. After passing a cornfield, it enters the shade of woods and emerges only briefly at a crossing of Tophet Swamp before it reaches the canoe launch on North Rd., a half-mile by pavement from the parking lot. Rising on a short hill, the

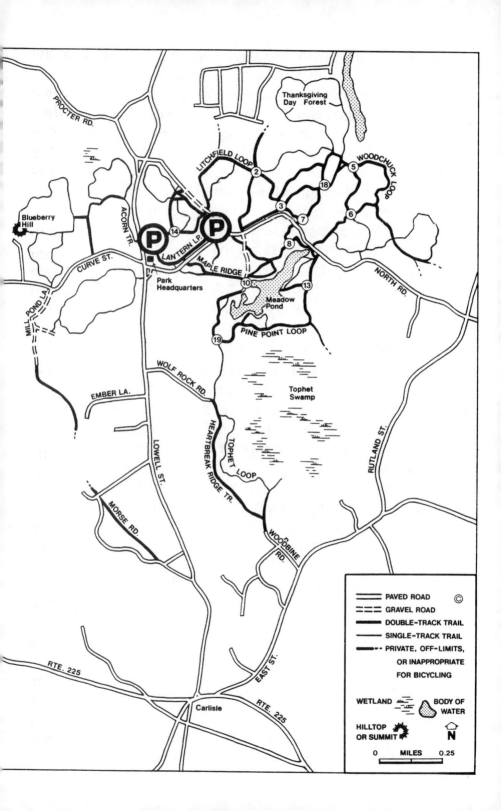

loop then returns to the meadows, a quarter-mile ahead.

Across the road from the canoe launch, the 1.1-mile **Woodchuck Trail** holds both bigger hills and bigger roots in equally beautiful scenery. The trail begins on the driveway to a cabin and continues through an area that was once a 1700's village called *The City* in its time. Sharp eyes will notice numerous cellarholes beside the trail. After rolling and curving through pine forest, it descends along the corridor of a gas pipeline, crosses a bridge over a brook, and rises to the open space of East Field. The Woodchuck Trail returns to the woods on the opposite side of the field and becomes a difficult ride up and then down one of the park's biggest hills before ending at North Rd. and the Litchfield Loop. The flatter, smoother **East Farm Trail** allows an alternate route from East Field to North Rd.

SINGLE-TRACKS:

Isolated single-tracks lie throughout the park but a 5-mile concentration of them west of Lowell St. has some of the best riding and holds a special attraction for mountain bikers since many of the paths are NEMBA creations. Look for a sign marking the **Acorn Trail** directly opposite the ski touring center parking lot. It leads through several fields to the rocky slopes of Blueberry Hill where mountain bikers must choose careful lines through a course of scattered stones. Several paths diverge along the way, including two that descend to Curve St. opposite Mill Pond La., a private road with a trail easement. Here cyclists can continue south on **Morse Road**, an old cart path that runs toward Sunset Rd., or head east on two difficult single-tracks that return to Lowell St. opposite the park headquarters building.

The mile-long **Heartbreak Ridge Trail** is another challenging single-track. Starting from the Pine Point Loop at intersection 19, it scrambles to the crest of an esker ridge and follows it south to Wolf Rock, then widens to double-track and enjoys a stable surface for the remaining 0.6 miles to Woodbine Rd. Expert riders will want to combine it with the **Tophet Loop**, a 0.8-mile side trip over the rocks and

82

roots of another esker with a NEMBA boardwalk at the midpoint.

The **Garrison** and **Deer Run** trails have some rocks to dodge at the park's eastern boundary. The Garrison Trail climbs from the Woodchuck Trail to the top of a small hill where a cellarhole marks the site of a small garrison built by settlers for defense against natives. Deer Run combines narrow spaces with rocks and roots in rideable terrain and crosses another NEMBA boardwalk at a wet area.

Thanksgiving Day Forest is owned by the town of Chelmsford and offers another mile or so of single-tracks near East Field. Head north across the pipeline corridor where several loops spread over rolling terrain.

DRIVING DIRECTIONS:

From Rte. 128/I-95 take Exit 31B and follow Rte. 225 west for 7 miles to Carlisle center. At the traffic circle turn right on Lowell St. and continue for 2 miles. To park at the farm, turn right on North Rd. or continue for another 100 yards to park at the ski touring center.

From I-495 take Exit 34 and follow Rte. 110 west to Chelmsford center. Follow Rte. 4 south for 1 mile, then bear right at a fork on Concord Rd. and continue for 2 miles. Park at the ski touring center on the left or, to park at the farm complex, turn left on North Rd. and look for the lot ahead on the left.

BIKE SHOPS:

The Bikeway Source, 111 South Rd., Bedford, Tel. (781) 275-7799

Bill & Andy's, 30 Chelmsford St. (Rte 110), Chelmsford, (978) 256-8811

Carr's Concord Sports, 69 Main St., Concord, (978) 369-4087

Chelmsford Cyclery, 7 Summer St., Chelmsford, (978) 256-1528

Pedal Power, 176 Great Rd. (Rte. 2A), Acton, (978) 263-3197

ADDITIONAL INFORMATION:

Great Brook Farm State Park, 984 Lowell St., Carlisle, MA 01741, Tel. (978) 369-6312

NEMBA, P.O. Box 2221, Acton, MA 01720-2221, www.nemba.org, Tel. (800) 57-NEMBA

11
Lowell-Dracut-Tyngsboro State Forest
Lowell

Few would expect to find such a mountain biking haven in the milltown that is America's industrial birthplace, but these 1,000 acres and 20 miles of trails sit ready and waiting to be discovered. Hidden in the hills above the Merrimack River at the corner of Lowell, Dracut, and Tyngsboro, this state forest will satisfy both novices and experts with its patchwork of options. And if you can look beyond the litter and debris, the scenery of beaver ponds, streams, and glacial boulders is a welcome complement.

BACKGROUND:

Lowell-Dracut-Tyngsboro State Forest is managed by the staff at nearby Lowell Heritage State Park and remains undeveloped so facilities are not present. The area gets relatively few visitors and its abandoned nature leaves it vulnerable as a site for dumping garbage, setting fires, and other unwanted activities. Signs at trailheads declare that motorized usage is prohibited but off-road dirt bikes and all-terrain vehicles frequent the forest and create new, unauthorized trails.

The Merrimack Valley chapter of NEMBA is focused on this state forest and welcomes you to join in the trail maintenance effort. For a schedule of future work days, check NEMBA's website at www.nemba.org.

TRAIL POLICIES:

Mountain biking is permitted on all trails. Riders are simply asked to travel at a safe speed and share the trails with others. Note that many of the trails leave the state forest for surrounding private land, and that boundaries are not always apparent.

ORIENTATION:

Few of the trails are named and no signs are present.

Newcomers must rely on the natural features of ponds and wetlands, a few old roads that form the core of the trail system, and surrounding paved roads to plot their courses. The trail network is interconnected with residential neighborhoods so many of the surrounding roads serve as public access points to the forest, although parking is provided only at the end of Trotting Park Rd.

The double-tracks, which are typically old farm roads dating from colonial times or even earlier, have mostly easy riding and the single-tracks, many made by the motorized crowd, have intermediate and difficult conditions.

GRAVEL ROADS:

Trotting Park Road serves as the main access point to the forest and also forms the backbone of the trail network. It begins as a residential street, passes through the gate at the trailhead parking lot, and continues into the woods with a paved surface that descends gradually as it turns through the trees. The road levels at the bottom and forks left, loosing its pavement for a short distance before emerging in a residential neighborhood in Tyngsboro at its northern end.

Carney Road is another of the forest's primary routes. Running perpendicular to Trotting Park Road, it begins a short distance from the parking lot, rises over a small hill and then descends to the edge of Spruce Swamp, a 150-acre wetland which is alive with birdlife and unique plants. The open expanse provides a nice view. The road's surface has eroded to become rocky in a few spots but tall, even stands of red pine give a peaceful feeling to the surrounding woods.

After one mile, Carney Road crosses the historic **Totman Road**, an old Indian trail which became a primary route for settlers to reach the northern wilderness from Boston in the 1700's. Both ends of Totman Road are paved and open to vehicle traffic but the gated midsection remains a simple, gravel road as it passes through the forest. Hills are mild so the pedaling is easy.

86

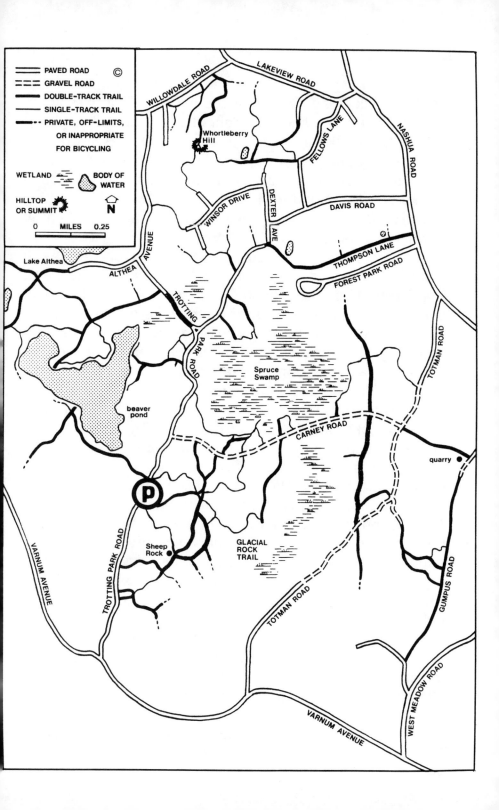

Mile-long **Thompson Lane** forks from the bottom of Trotting Park Road. Its surface is paved until it passes the end of Dexter Ave. and then degrades to a gravelly trail that traces the backyards of houses along Forest Park Rd. Thompson Lane follows a corridor of land to an obscure trailhead on Nashua Rd., identifiable by a row of granite blocks beside the trail. Circling Spruce Swamp on Trotting Park Road, Thompson Lane, Totman Road, and Carney Road makes an easy, 3.5-mile tour.

Two trails continue past Totman Road to reach **Gumpus Road**, an old wagon track lined with stone walls. Connecting Mammoth Rd. in Dracut with West Meadow Rd. in Lowell, this route's narrower width and eroded spots keep rider's on their guard. It follows the state forest's eastern boundary alongside an apartment complex for part of the way and passes a former granite quarry which has now flooded with water to form a small pond.

The western part of the forest holds several easy double-tracks but most are interrupted by either private property or the flooded area of a large **beaver pond**. An easy woods road leaves Trotting Park Road at a sign marking the Historic Pawtucket Indian Site, a permit area designated for use by the Greater Lowell Indian Cultural Association, and runs for a half-mile before disappearing beneath the water. The parallel trail leaving the end of Althea Ave. is disguised as a private driveway but serves as a public entrance to the forest near the shore of **Lake Althea**. It eventually hits private land but two trails link the trail to the Indian site.

The double-tracks ascending 363' **Whortleberry Hill** are not so easy. Isolated at the northern bounds of the forest but accessible by numerous public roads, these trails offer strenuous climbs and a few obstacles to complicate the effort. The route starting from Willowdale Rd. is the toughest, climbing to the top in a half-mile of switchbacks. The summit has no view but a small pond just below it is a pretty spot to stop and rest.

SINGLE-TRACKS:

Exciting single-tracks exist throughout this state forest, usually in nameless fragments that link otherwise dead end double-tracks. Some of the best are concentrated near the trailhead parking lot and include the paths tracing the southern edge of Spruce Swamp and continuing to Totman Road. The **Glacial Rock Trail** is tight and quick, weaving through trees and rolling with small hills and turns. It passes slabs of exposed bedrock and a collection of glacial erratics, huge boulders left from the Ice Age which are now splitting apart with time. One of the largest is Sheep Rock where according to folklore a herd of sheep took refuge and was snowbound for several days during a severe blizzard in the 1800's. Sharp eyes will notice the inscription dedicating the boulder to the memory of George Carney who farmed this land at the time.

DRIVING DIRECTIONS:

From I-495 take Exit 38 for Rte. 38 and drive north for 2 miles. Continue for 0.2 miles beyond a rotary and, where Rte. 38 turns right at a traffic signal, stay straight on the VFW Hwy. After 2.4 miles bear right at a flashing yellow light on Varnum Ave., drive for 1.9 miles, and turn right on Trotting Park Rd. Park in the lot at the end, being careful to not block the gate.

BIKE SHOPS:

Foxco, 1595 Bridge St. (Rte. 38), Dracut, Tel. (978) 458-9261

Northeast Sports and Cycle Center, 1595 Lakeview Ave., Dracut, Tel. (978) 957-6199

ADDITIONAL INFORMATION:

Lowell-Dracut-Tyngsboro State Forest, c/o Lowell Heritage State Park, 25 Shattuck St., Lowell, MA 01852, Tel. (978) 453-1950

12
Groton Memorial Town Forest
Groton

Tucked in a corner of Groton's rolling countryside, this mountain biking hot-spot holds some of the region's most exciting single-tracks. A wild terrain of abrupt hills together with miles of motorcycle paths make the Groton Memorial Town Forest a popular place for riders looking for a challenge but a group of mellower double-tracks makes it equally appealing for easy biking.

BACKGROUND:

The Groton Memorial Town Forest originated with a gift of land in 1922 and the 500-acre tract is dedicated to the town's citizens who died in World War I. The property is a registered tree farm and managed for the cultivation of forest products, and portions having been logged recently. It is one of Groton's largest and most beautiful pieces of protected land and recreational use of the trails is encouraged. Hunting is permitted in season and is most popular in the late fall.

The town forest is described in this chapter together with two other nearby properties, one a parcel of town conservation land and the other a property of the New England Forestry Foundation. Both are open for passive recreation.

TRAIL POLICIES:

Regulations for use of the trails at the town forest are relatively relaxed and the policy is not expected to change. The trails are open to both passive and motorized recreational use and the woods roads beyond the parking lot are open to cars. Motorcycles have long been welcome throughout property and have caused severe erosion at many points where the trails encounter steep slopes and sandy soils. Try to minimize this damage when you ride.

Two parking areas are shown on the accompanying map, one that serves the town forest and another that serves neighboring lands. Signs denote the names of most of the double-tracks but single-tracks remain unnamed and unmarked. A river and a railroad provide obvious boundaries for much of the trail system but unmarked private property exists along the town forest's northwest boundary.

Town Forest Road continues for a mile beyond the parking area at the stone monument. It begins with a quarter-mile of slight uphill, forks right and levels for a short distance, then makes a gradual descent to the open corridor of the abandoned railroad. An easy ride, most of this distance enjoys a smooth, sandy finish but a few of the downhills have eroded areas with loose rocks. The tall, straight trunks of surrounding white pines add distinction to the trip as they rise like huge columns into the forest canopy.

Town Forest Road accesses other double-tracks that offer more easy cruising. **Wharton Road** forks left after the first quarter-mile and takes a straight, flat course past the Dead River, once a bend in the Nashua River and now an algae-covered backwater. This sharp turn and the former peninsula known as the Neck became severed from the river in 1751 by a flood which reportedly swept bridges away. Wharton Road follows the edge of a steep banking high above the stillwater and then turns, rises over a low ridge, and drops to a five-way intersection after 0.6 miles.

The main flow of traffic continues downhill from this point on **Priest Bridge Road** which bends between two small hills on an easy, half-mile course to the railroad tracks. It is possible to turn right and follow a narrow path beside the tracks northward for almost a mile to connect with the end of Town Forest Road, creating a 3.3-mile loop from the monument. No longer in use, this railroad runs between the neighboring towns of Ayer and Townsend and follows the

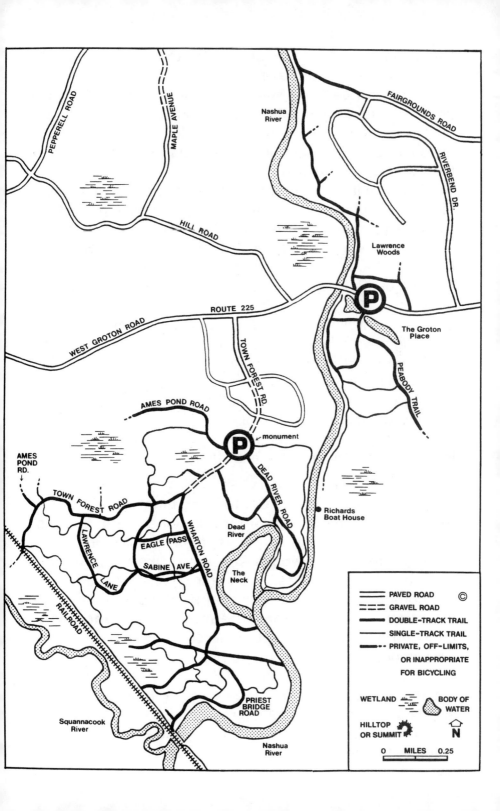

Squannacook River, a quiet stream named with the Algonquin word for *place of salmon*.

Lawrence Lane, **Sabine Avenue**, and **Eagle Pass** are easy alternatives within this loop offering flat terrain and open surfaces. A similar ride, Dead River Road is a short option leading from the monument past the Dead River to the shore of the Nashua.

Cross the river on Rte. 225 to find several more miles of gentle double-tracks. **The Groton Place**, a property of the New England Forestry Foundation, has a formal entrance gate and welcomes visitors with a park-like setting of open spaces and elegant stone benches. The tranquil scenery of the Nashua River makes it an excellent place for a picnic. The **Peabody Trail** begins at the main gate and forks left as it rises to the interior of the property, eventually reaching private land. Several other paths intersect on the right and join the Peabody to a fun shoreline route that returns to the trailhead.

Across the road, **Lawrence Woods** is a parcel of town conservation land and offers another scenic, but short, tour along the water. Tall pines and a cushion of needles lend peace and quiet to the easy trails.

SINGLE-TRACKS:

The highlight at Groton for most riders is the excitement to be found on the nameless single-tracks. Created by off-road motorcycles, these challenging paths spread through the woods in a dreamlike maze of tight spaces, corkscrew turns, and abrupt transitions. Many of the corners are banked, allowing extra control for riders negotiating the constant stream of twists and turns. Exposed tree roots disrupt some sections but others are silky smooth.

The single-tracks south of Lawrence Lane are among the most difficult as they tackle some impossibly steep slopes and a roller coaster of smaller ones. Be prepared to encounter sudden up- and downhill transitions in the dramatic terrain.

94

Flatter single-tracks can be found near Eagle Pass and Sabine Avenue where intermediate-level rides await with narrow widths, winding courses, and some tree roots making the trail surfaces bumpy.

Other intermediate single-tracks start near the monument. One begins at Dead River Road and follows the banks of the Dead River and the Nashua back to the monument, forming a short loop that bobs along the water's edge with a playful series of bumps and dips. A second loop from the monument involves about a mile of single-track running between Town Forest Road and Ames Pond Road where a few short hills spice the pedaling.

DRIVING DIRECTIONS:

From I-495 take Exit 31 and follow Rte. 119 west for 7 miles to Groton center. Turn left on Rte. 225 west/Rte. 111 south and drive for 0.6 miles to where the two split, then turn right on Rte. 225. To park at the Groton Place, continue for 0.7 miles to the gate on the left-hand side. To park at the monument, continue for 1.2 miles, turn left on Town Forest Rd., and look for the monument a half-mile ahead at the edge of the woods.

BIKE SHOPS:

Gamaches Cyclery, 65 Laurel St. (Rte. 12), Fitchburg, Tel. (978) 343-3140

Gear Works Cyclery, 510 N. Main St. (Rte. 12), Leominster, Tel. (978) 534-2453

O'Neil's Bicycle Shop, 39 Mechanic St., Leominster, Tel. (978) 537-6464

Pedal Power, 176 Great Rd. (Rte. 2A/119), Acton, Tel. (978) 263-3197

ADDITIONAL INFORMATION:

Groton Conservation Committee, P.O. Box 669, Groton, MA 01450

New England Forestry Foundation, 85 Newbury St., Boston, MA 02116

13
Townsend State Forest
Townsend

Even though the many tire tracks and chainring marks along these 20 miles of trails suggest that mountain biking is Townsend State Forest's most popular activity, it is likely that you will have the place to yourself. Footsteps from the New Hampshire border, these ledgy hills and challenging single-tracks have little to offer novice mountain bikers and are geared instead toward intermediate and advanced riders.

BACKGROUND:

The origin of this 2800-acre preserve lies in a natural disaster. After a forest fire had destroyed much of the area in 1927, the state purchased the acreage in the early 1930's under the Reforestation Act and helped to establish a camp of the Civilian Conservation Corps during the Great Depression. The group planted many of the trees which stand today. Given the swimming and camping attractions at nearby Willard Brook State Forest, this property has remained free of much public attention and, except for its trails and unmarked parking lot, is completely undeveloped.

TRAIL POLICIES:

The forest is managed by the staff at Willard Brook State Forest who ask mountain bikers to use common sense when riding by respecting other trail users and being sensitive to trail erosion. Motorcycles are not permitted on the trails but nonetheless appear to make frequent use of them. Hunting is a popular activity at Townsend State Forest and all visitors are advised to take appropriate precautions, especially during deer season in the late fall.

ORIENTATION:

Almost all the trails are unnamed and unmarked so navigating this maze will be a challenge for the first time.

97

Generic *State Property* notices posted along the property boundaries are the only visible signs. The majority of the double-tracks have a north-south orientation, with higher elevations being toward the north, and originate on public roads which bound the trail system to the south and east. Pay careful attention to the map and plot your progress as you go.

In general, most double-tracks have hills and exposed rocks and tree roots which make them intermediate-level riding, while the single-tracks encounter steeper hills and bigger rocks for difficult riding.

DOUBLE-TRACKS:

Tall white pines and a neat row of boulders surround the parking lot on Dudley Rd. where **Graves Road** is the only trail leading into the woods. It starts as a flat ride through a stand of pines, emerges in a clearing beside Loup Pond, and crosses two inlet brooks. Forking left at the next intersection, the trail rises into dissiduous forest with a rockier surface and continues uphill for most of the next mile with intermediate conditions. Halfway up this hill it narrows to single-track but the treadway is smooth except for avoidable rocks. The elevation gain is mixed with some brief downhills near the top.

Two nameless double-tracks depart from Dudley Road near the parking lot and head to the higher elevations at the New Hampshire state line, 2 miles to the north. These intermediate-level trails have rocks and roots to negotiate as well as a few mudholes.

Fessenden Hill Road is an unmaintained public road linking Townsend with its northern neighbor, Brookline, New Hampshire, over the course of 2 miles. It gets occasional four-wheel-drive use and erosion has left loose rocks on a few of the slopes but most of its distance is a relatively smooth ride. Tree branches reach into the space of the road narrowing it to a width for barely a car. It starts at Rte. 13, passes a few homes, and then enters deep woods as its

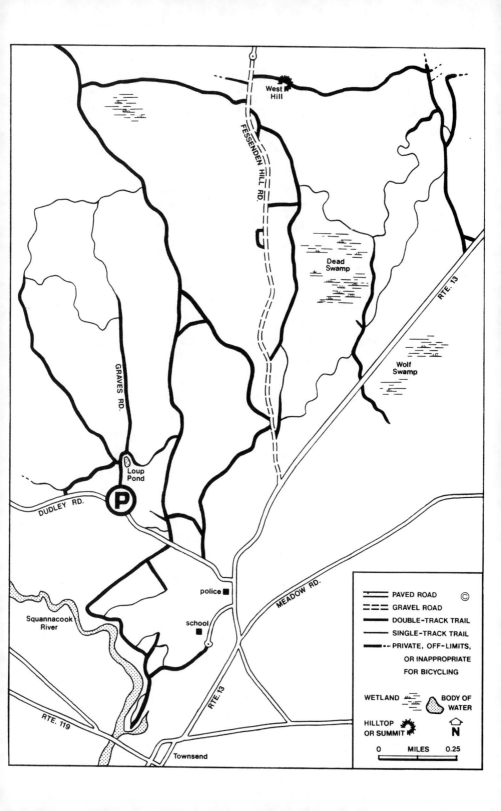

West
Hill

FESSENDEN HILL RD.

Dead
Swamp

RTE. 13

GRAVES RD.

Wolf
Swamp

Loup
Pond

P

DUDLEY RD.

MEADOW RD.

police

school

Squannacook
River

RTE. 13

RTE. 119

Townsend

PAVED ROAD ©
GRAVEL ROAD
DOUBLE-TRACK TRAIL
SINGLE-TRACK TRAIL
PRIVATE, OFF-LIMITS,
OR INAPPROPRIATE
FOR BICYCLING

WETLAND   BODY OF
                 WATER

HILLTOP   N
OR SUMMIT

0   MILES   0.25

climbs to the north.

Mountain bikers can combine several of these intermediate-level double-tracks for a 5-mile tour of the forest. Beginning at the parking lot, follow Graves Road past Loup Pond and up the hill to its endpoint on an unnamed double-track originating on Dudley Rd. Turn left on this trail and continue north through a combination of ups and downs and several wet spots that collect rainwater across the entire width of the trail. After a half-mile, a short distance before the New Hampshire line, turn right at the first intersection and ride eastward. Much of this trail is smooth and easy but isolated sections of erosion or mud add difficulty. After a final uphill scramble, turn right on Fessenden Road and enjoy the mostly downhill ride to Rte. 13, watching for loose rocks on the slopes. Turn right on the pavement and then right on Dudley Rd. to complete the loop and return to the parking lot.

Look for the gentlest terrain and smoothest trails south of Dudley Rd. near the **Squannacook River**. Partly on state forest and partly on town-owned land, this cluster of trails offers peaceful woods and some worthwhile views over the water flow. Tree roots ripple the trails in places and a few trails diverge to climb a nearby knoll, but most of the riding is easy.

SINGLE-TRACKS:

It is the single-tracks that make Townsend State Forest a special place. Twisting through a rugged landscape of boulders and ledge, these paths attract a steady following and are the main course for mountain bikers hungry for a challenging ride.

The most difficult one lies on the hill above the main parking lot. Following Graves Road, turn left at the first intersection and then immediately right on a double-track with a gradual uphill grade. A steady climb, this trail is mostly intermediate riding but a few difficult spots exist where rocks, roots, and mudholes slow the pedaling. After crossing a small bridge near the 1-mile mark the trail splits into two single-tracks that both return to the upper end of Graves Road. A right turn at this intersection sends bikers on the forest's most technical trail, a boneyard of rocks with some short, steep uphills. This path is faint and most bicycle traffic keeps left on the more rideable option that offers a satisfying combination of turns and obstacles, although a few brief pitches could prove to be too steep to pedal.

More single-tracks await on the granite knolls above Dead Swamp east of Fessenden Hill Road. The two closest to Rte. 13 are an especially good ride as they traverse a hillside on a carefully laid route that weaves through trees and slips between slabs of ledge. Slight views through the trees can be enjoyed at points along the way.

DRIVING DIRECTIONS:

From I-495 take Exit 31 and follow Rte. 119 west for 14.5 miles to Townsend center. Turn right at the traffic signal on Rte. 31 and drive north for 0.8 miles, then turn left at the police station on Dudley Rd. Look for the parking lot a half-mile ahead on the right.

BIKE SHOPS:

Gamache Cyclery, 65 Laurel St. (Rte. 12), Fitchburg, Tel. (978) 343-3140

Gear Works Cyclery, 510 North Main St. (Rte. 12), Leominster, Tel. (978) 534-2453

O'Neil's Bicycle Shop, 39 Mechanic St., Leominster, Tel. (978) 537-6464

ADDITIONAL INFORMATION:

Townsend State Forest, c/o Willard Brook State Forest, Rte. 119, West Townsend, MA 01474, Tel. (978) 597-8802

14
Leominster State Forest
Westminster

In the shadow of Mount Wachusett, this 4,300-acre tract is an outdoor adventurer's dream of rock climbing cliffs, fishing and swimming ponds, and miles of hiking and mountain biking trails. A 10-mile network of fire roads allows easy and intermediate riding and many more miles of twisty single-tracks hold difficult conditions.

BACKGROUND:

In the late 1800's this was a place called Notown, a settlement of small farms that survived only until the early 1900's, when the state acquired the properties and established this preserve. Today the forest is an especially popular spot in summer when its sandy beach and shady picnic area are the main attractions. It is also well known for deer hunting so mountain bikers are discouraged from using these trails during the late fall, except on Sundays when hunting is prohibited by law.

TRAIL POLICIES:

Mountain biking is not permitted everywhere. Several trails, mostly in the area of Crow Hill Pond and Crow Hill, are reserved for hiking and marked as such with wooden signs. Bicycles are permitted on all other trails and fire roads.

This policy is a major improvement from that of years past when bikes (along with motorcycles) became prohibited from the single-tracks. The efforts of the New England Mountain Bike Association (NEMBA) and its energetic Wachusett chapter have returned mountain bikes to most of these paths through a successful series of trail maintenance projects aimed at restoring eroded slopes and alleviating damage to wet areas. Although the ban on motorized usage remains, the future for both mountain biking and more trail work looks bright. Volunteer if you can.

Several parking lots along Rte. 31 serve the forest's various user groups. Mountain bikers are advised to park at the lot at the end of Rocky Pond Road where access to multi-use trails is direct. Be careful not to block the trailhead gate as work crews and emergency vehicles always need access.

The majority of fire roads are named and marked by wooden signs, but the winding single-tracks are unnamed and unmarked and their convoluted routes can be disorienting. Note that several trails leave the state forest land for private property along the eastern boundary and, although they are frequented by mountain bikers, are not included in this description. For a more complete map of these outlying trails stop at Forest Headquarters on Rte. 31.

Rocky Pond Road bisects the state forest and serves as a backbone to the trail system. One of the area's oldest, the road is a manageable ride for all abilities although the surface is a bit rough where it meets several hills. From the trailhead gate at Rte. 31, the ride starts with a 0.7-mile climb past several intersecting trails on a steady incline to a saddle between two hills where an old granite post marks the Princeton-Westminster town line.

The name changes to **Parmenter Road** when it reaches the nearby border of Leominster and descends in step-like pitches for a quarter-mile to Rocky Pond, visible through the trees on the left. The road continues its descent for another quarter-mile beyond Rocky Pond, crosses a brook, and rises to a four-way intersection in a pine forest. A final hill climb, the most strenuous of this 2.4-mile ride, marks the last half-mile to Elm St.

Secondary fire roads that are classified here as double-tracks branch at numerous points. Heading north, 0.8-mile **Fenton Road** starts beside a stand of red pine,

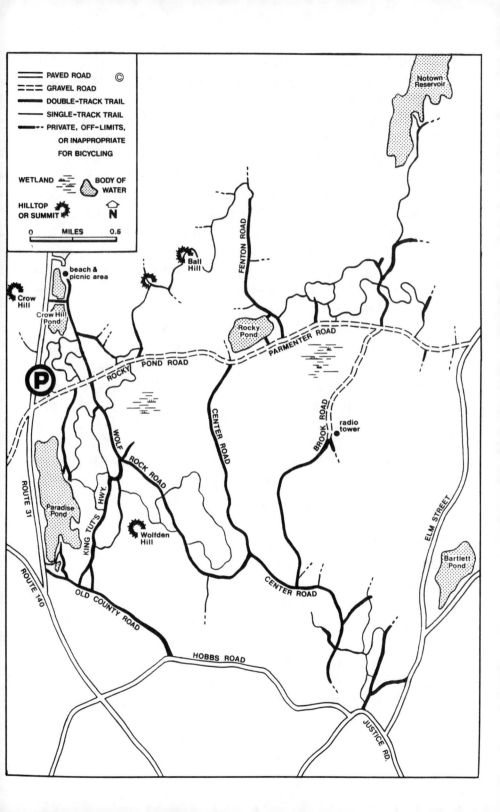

drops to the shore of Rocky Pond with a view across the water to Mount Wachusett, then traverses a hill and ends in a jungle of mountain laurel bushes.

To the south, **Wolf Rock Road**, **Center Road**, and **Brook Road** combine to form an intermediate-level, 5.6-mile loop. A quarter-mile up Rocky Pond Road from the trailhead, take the second right turn on Wolf Rock Road. After an initial uphill scramble on a loose surface, the road rolls with a combination of ups and downs alternating its surface between rough and smooth. It forks left at an intersection after a half-mile, then reaches the top of Wolfden Hill and begins to descend, slightly at first and more swiftly toward the bottom. Several of these final pitches are eroded and deserve caution.

Turn right on Center Road at the bottom and then take the next left on Brook Road after a third of a mile. Lined with mountain laurel bushes, Brook Road starts in the shade of trees, climbs the slope of a low hill to a radio tower, then descends to a stand of pines on Parmenter Road. Turn left at this intersection to return to Rte. 31, 1.9 miles away. Short-cutting on Center Road reduces the loop to 3.9 miles.

King Tut's Highway forks from Wolf Rock Road with a fairly smooth, gentle ride until it drops on several rocky pitches near the southern end of Paradise Pond. It links **Old County Road**, a forgotten town road that is an intermediate ride from exposed rocks.

SINGLE-TRACKS:

Unfortunately the single-tracks have no names so any trail descriptions are inherently vague.

Some of the most exciting riding awaits just north of the parking lot where about 2 miles of paths turn and bob in a wooded area of small bulges and hollows. The nearby path running northward from Rocky Pond Road along the shore of **Crow Hill Pond** is a difficult, rocky ride to the beach area, where restrooms are open during the summer.

Pedaling to the two tops of **Ball Hill** is a strenuous trip. The half-mile incline begins at Rocky Pond Road with

106

double-track width, narrows to single-track, then gets rough with rocks. Reaching a T-intersection at the first summit, mountain bikers can turn right and descend to another intersection, turn left, and then climb several steep pitches to reach the second summit. The trail then loops back and descends for most of the next 1.2 miles to its endpoint at another T-intersection. Turning right, it is less than a quarter-mile to the end of Fenton Road.

East of Fenton Road lies an area of single-tracks nicknamed *Jane Fonda*. Fewer rocks bulge through the soils here so bicycle tires roll more freely and riders can focus their attention on the exciting mix of small hills and quick turns. A rocky, often wet trail runs northward from this area along the state forest boundary to a scenic point of land in **Notown Reservoir**, 1.4 miles from Rocky Pond Rd.

Single-tracks wind through the terrain at the southwestern corner of the state forest with the same zeal. The loop located between Center Road and the southern end of Wolf Rock Road struggles over rocks in places but takes a playful, turning course through the trees on the eastern slope of Wolfden Hill. Across Wolf Rock Road, a number of well-worn paths contend with the rocky slopes above Paradise Pond in difficult, direct-line pitches.

DRIVING DIRECTIONS:
From Rte. 2 take Exit 28 and follow Rte. 31 south for 2.6 miles and look for the gravel surface of Rocky Pond Rd. on the left. Park in the lot being careful not to block the gate.

BIKE SHOPS:
Gamaches Cyclery, 65 Laurel St. (Rte. 12), Fitchburg, Tel. (978) 343-3140
Gear Works Cyclery, 510 N. Main St. (Rte. 12), Leominster, Tel. (978) 534-2453
O'Neil's Bicycle Shop, 39 Mechanic St., Leominster, Tel. (978) 537-6464

ADDITIONAL INFORMATION:
Leominster State Forest, Rte. 31, Westminster, MA 01473, Tel. (978) 874-2303

15
Stow Town Forest
Stow

Known for its farm stands, apple orchards, and many golf courses, Stow is a popular place to enjoy the pleasures of the countryside. Less known is the pocket of mountain biking trails at the town forest where several miles of easy woods roads meander through peaceful forests along the banks of a lazy river. Smaller than most places to ride, Stow is ideal for an afternoon tour or a short workout.

BACKGROUND:

This acreage was purchased in the early 1960's as Stow's first conservation land. It remains a simple place, free of amenities other than the parking lot, trailhead sign, and 10 miles of trails.

TRAIL POLICIES:

Stow's conservation commission welcomes passive uses at the property but prohibits motor vehicles of any kind. The area is open only during daylight hours. Mountain bikers should observe the standard rules of etiquette by riding only when the ground is dry, announcing your presence to avoid startling others, and being ready to yield the trail.

ORIENTATION:

Trail signs are not present but the conservation commission has named many routes and marked them with individually colored tree blazes, although these have faded and become difficult to notice.

Note that private property surrounds the forest and that peripheral trails leave the public land at many points. Although some abutters have posted their land with *No Trespassing* signs, the town forest's boundaries are not readily identifiable so pay careful attention to the trail map.

The double-track trails are generally flat and easy

riding and the single-tracks are hillier and more challenging.

DOUBLE-TRACKS:

A green, metal gate at the end of Bradley La. marks the public trailhead and the beginning of **Forest Lane**, a smooth woods road which descends briefly to a bridge over Assabet Brook. Here, barely noticeable beneath the undergrowth, is the foundation of Stow's first sawmill which originated in 1681 and provided the town with lumber for 150 years. Forest Lane then bears left at a fork, rises on a short hill, and continues for a half-mile before reaching a gravel pit beside private property. Flat terrain and a smooth surface allow easy rolling.

Three main trails intersect Forest Lane. The first and smoothest option is **Fletcher Lane** which forks to the right after Assabet Brook and follows the edge of a wetland along the northern boundary of the town forest. Fletcher Lane joins the ends of two routes running to the south, the **Gardner Hill Trail** and a trail following a buried **AT&T cable**. Choosing the Gardner Hill Trail, marked by faint orange blazes, brings a gradual uphill slope at the beginning and a bumpy ride from the tree roots stretching across its half-mile-long path to the scout area. Following the straight route of the AT&T cable is a smoother option with a couple of short, abrupt hills to climb.

The second major trail intersecting Forest Lane is the **White Birch Trail**, marked by white blazes. Long tree roots grasp its entire width in places and jolt an otherwise tranquil, 0.8-mile ride to Timberidge Rd. where the trail passes between two homes to reach the pavement. It crosses both the Gardner Hill Trail and the AT&T cable on the way.

The **King's Cove Trail** forms the last intersection with Forest Lane near the gravel pit. This easy woods road runs for a mile to the White Birch Trail near Timberidge Rd. with a smooth, sandy finish and some of the town forest's prettiest scenery. It passes deep, dark stands of white pine as well as the shore of King's Cove, a bay in the Assabet River at the forest's southern boundary. Crow Island, visible across

110

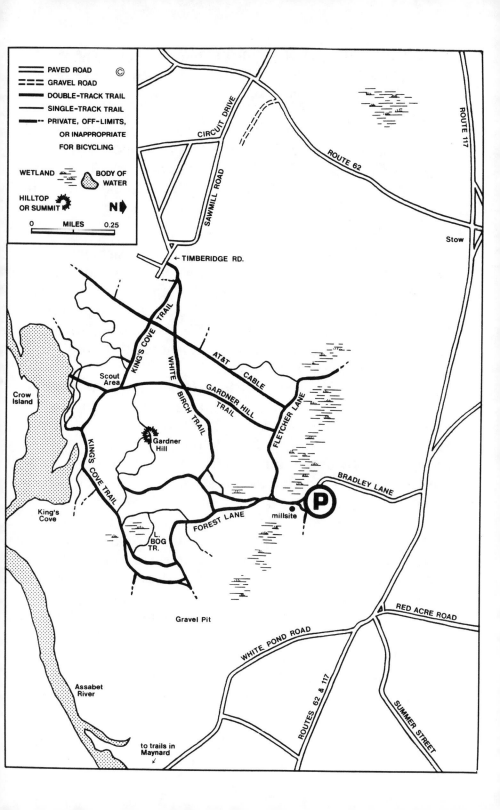

the water, is the site of a small airstrip for ultralights which buzz over the town forest's treetops on fair-weather days.

An easy, 2.5-mile loop can be made on these woods roads for an introduction to the area. From the parking lot take Forest Lane for a third of a mile, turn right on the White Birch Trail and continue straight to the end where it merges with the King's Cove Trail, near Timberidge Rd. Turn hard left and follow King's Cove Trail for a mile to the end, then turn left on Forest Lane to return to the trailhead.

SINGLE-TRACKS:

A limited amount of single-track riding exists for those looking for more challenge. Paths such as the **Little Bog Trail** offer narrow, curvey courses through the woods with occasional logs and rocks to hop. A cluster of single-tracks between the river and the AT&T cable at the forest's southern extreme offer a worthwhile cruise through the woods and over a few stone walls.

Pedaling up 334' **Gardner Hill** is the area's most challenging ride and should be attempted on the more gradual, eastern approach. Begin from Forest Lane on the White Birch Trail and, at the first hard-right turn, continue straight on an unblazed double-track which rises on a gradual slope. Rocks break the surface and tree branches reach into the space of the trail along this section. Within the first quarter-mile it dips and joins a single-track entering on the left from the King's Cove Trail, then narrows and begins to climb more quickly. At this point the trail forks, each branch heading to the top with a steady incline, plenty of rocks, and a scattering of logs. The top of the hill is tree-covered and has no view. The path continues straight down the western slope to the Gardner Hill Trail with an eroded and steep pitch, so plan on walking the bike if you travel this section. The total distance over the hill is a half-mile.

DRIVING DIRECTIONS:

From Rte. 2 exit at Rte. 62 in Concord and drive west for 6.5 miles, passing through the centers of West Concord and Maynard. Look for Bradley La. on the left, a short distance beyond the Stow Shopping Center. Park in the lot at the end of Bradley La., 0.4 miles ahead.

From I-495 take Exit 27 and follow Rte. 117 east for 5 miles to Stow center at the intersection of Rte. 62. Continue on Rte. 117 east for another 0.7 miles and turn right on Bradley La., just before the Stow Shopping Center. Park in the lot at the end of Bradley La., 0.4 miles ahead.

PUBLIC TRANSPORTATION:

The Fitchburg line stops at South Acton. From the station, turn left on Central St. and ride for a third of a mile, then turn left on Martin St. and continue to a five-way intersection. Turn right at this point on Liberty St. (which becomes Red Acre Rd. in Stow) and ride for 2.2 miles to the end, turn right on Rte. 117, then left on Bradley La.. Total distance is 3.7 miles.

BIKE SHOPS:

Ray & Sons Cyclery, 183 Main St. (Rte. 62), Maynard, Tel. (978) 897-8121

Yankee Pedaler, 141 Main St. (Rte. 62), Hudson, Tel. (978) 568-9070

U.S.G.S. MAPS:

Hudson Quadrangle, Maynard Quadrangle

ADDITIONAL INFORMATION:

Stow Conservation Commission, Stow Town Building, Stow, MA 01775

16
Weston Conservation Lands
Weston

The Weston Forest and Trail Association maintains an impressive 65 miles of trails on over 2,200 acres of conservation lands and easements on private properties. The conditions for mountain biking are mostly easy and intermediate.

BACKGROUND:

Weston's sprawling trail network is a tribute to early planning and open space preservation. Formed in 1955, the Weston Forest and Trail Association was one of the state's first local land conservation groups and, together with the Weston Conservation Commission, has provided much of the foresight and energy needed to establish what the town enjoys today. The group also schedules trail walks, offers lectures on land conservation, and maintains trails. Membership in the Weston Forest and Trail Association is not limited to Weston residents and helps to support these efforts.

TRAIL POLICIES:

Signs at many trail/road intersections urge visitors to *Respect the woods*. Mountain bikers should take these words to heart by being sensitive to trail surfaces, courteous to other trail users, and appreciative of the natural places that they visit. Bicycles are permitted on Weston's trails only when the ground is firm and dry, and are excluded during wet weather and during spring thaw from March 1 through April 15. To minimize trail impacts, bicyclists are encouraged to use the town's double-tracks and to refrain from riding on hillsides. The various trail user groups in Weston have coexisted to date but authorities warn that the multi-use policy can easily be changed if complaints arise. In short, pedal *very* softly.

Trail easements allow the public to cross some private properties at certain points and are a special privilege for hikers, joggers, horseback riders, and bicyclists who can reach otherwise distant places. Since many of these connections wrap intricately around the homes, backyards, and driveways of local residents follow the trails carefully and show proper respect for those who live nearby.

ORIENTATION:

Few trails are named but each is clearly marked by white, aluminum tree tags with a green arrow pointing in the direction of travel. Where public trails end beside private property these markers point downward to the ground. The markers are especially helpful in identifying the location of trailheads at roadways since many paths are narrow and obscured by foliage. Some also display the intersection numbers and letters that are shown on the map, and it should be noted that these numbers and letters are repeated numerous times in various parts of the town's trail network. The Weston Forest and Trail Association sells a large and accurate map of all the town's conservation lands and trails at the Engineer's Office in the basement of Weston Town Hall.

Two trailhead parking lots are shown on the map but smaller places also exist. Neighborhoods of trails lie throughout the town and numerous linkages provide plenty of options for long rides. Since many areas are vast and densely packed, follow the map carefully and note the labeled trail intersections that you pass and the roads that you cross.

DOUBLE-TRACKS:

Almost all of Weston's double-track trails have easy biking conditions. Beginning at the **College Conservation Area**, a small network branches from the trail leading past a metal gate beside two tennis courts. This trail crosses a field and then splits, with the right-hand option heading south to Merriam St. and the left-hand option heading north to the end of Juniper Rd. The terrain is generally flat and the scenery includes forests, meadows, and a small pond.

Located across Concord Rd. a short distance from the parking lot, the **Dickson Memorial Riding Ring** serves as the main entrance to Weston's largest piece of open space, which is used frequently for horseback riding so bicyclists should pedal cautiously. Follow the dirt road downhill from the ring and into the woods to intersection 2, where it forks. The left-hand option is a flat and easy, 0.6-mile ride past intersections **F** and **E** to Warren Ave. while the right-hand choice is a 1.2-mile pedal to Rte. 20 in the equally mellow terrain of intersections **3** through **9**. The trail forking right at intersection **6** leads to **French Field**, a break in the forest where a few acres of grass provide a nice spot for picnicking.

Another pocket of double-tracks lies at the corner of town north of Sudbury Rd. To find it, follow Sudbury Rd. west from Concord Rd. and look for a woods road entering on the right, just after a residence and just before the Wayland town line. Here a mile or so of double-tracks explore rolling terrain and quiet forest along the course of intersections **1** through **8**.

Across town, a 2-mile trail circles **Weston Reservoir** with mostly easy mountain biking, although the surface is rough at a few points where erosion has exposed rocks. The reservoir is a water supply and protected by a chainlink fence that prevents visitors from reaching the shoreline but its pretty views are a nice complement to the riding. Nearby parking makes it easily accessible.

West of **Regis College** is another neighborhood of easy double-tracks. These grassy wagon roads have obstacle-free riding in forest scenery and are accessible from a variety of surrounding roads. Named for its great western vista, **Sunset Corner** offers a window on the horizon that stretches to New Hampshire's Mt. Monadnock on a clear day. Mt. Wachusett cuts the horizon some 30 miles to the west.

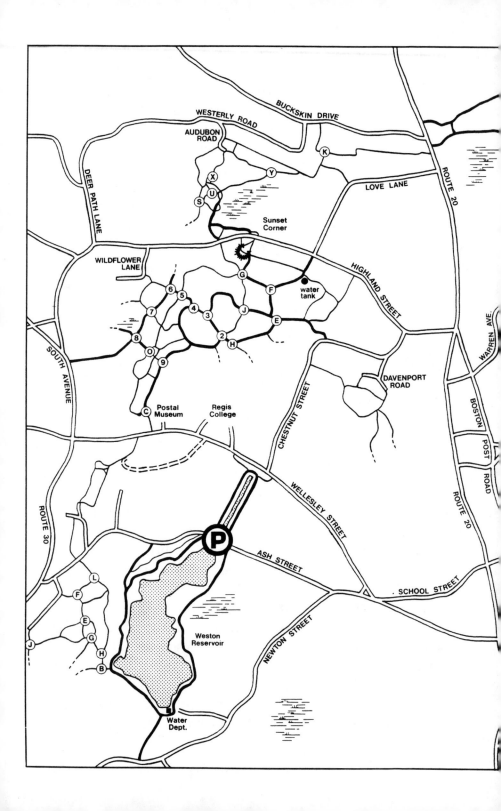

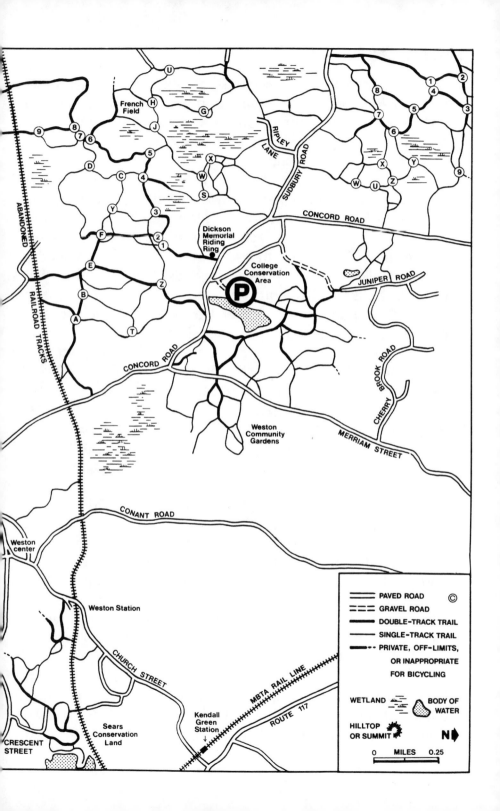

Weston's countless miles of single-track trails have mostly intermediate conditions for mountain biking. Slipping narrowly through natural features, they wander into quiet corners of town and explore surroundings that are typical in far more remote locations.

The College Conservation Area trailhead is the best starting point for a single-track ride. East of the parking lot, a tangle of intermediate-level paths weaves through the woods and extends across Merriam St. to the **Weston Community Gardens** with tree roots causing a bumpy ride. Expect mellow slopes and a few wet spots too. The pocket of trails between Concord Rd. and Sudbury Rd. can be reached via paths from Juniper Rd. near the trailhead and ranges from intermediate to difficult riding.

More roots await across Concord Rd. on single-tracks in the area of the Dickson Memorial Riding Ring. These trails keep to fairly flat terrain except for those in the cluster near intersections **X**, **W**, and **S** where a small hillside exists. Although most get an intermediate rating, a few trails have stone wall crossings and wet spots that could require brief carries and the segment linking intersections **4**, **C**, and **D** is rough with exposed rocks.

Heading south, a single-track leaves Rte. 20 between Buckskin Dr. and Love La. following a long, narrow strip of conservation land to link more options. This trail starts with an easy ride beside the back yards of nearby residences and gradually becomes rougher with tree roots and debris as it approaches Audubon Rd. Cross Highland St. and climb over the hillside at **Sunset Corner** to find several more miles of intermediate-level single-tracks mingling with the double-tracks behind **Regis College**.

The small collection of single-tracks near **Weston Reservoir** hold an engaging mix of obstacles as they explore livelier terrain near intersections **E**, **G**, **H**, and **B**. These paths wind through trees and bump over exposed rocks.

120

From Rte. 128 (I-95) take Exit 26 and follow Rte. 20 west for 1.1 miles. To reach the College Conservation Area, bear right on Boston Post Rd. where it splits from Rte. 20, following signs for Weston center. Turn right on Concord Rd. after a half-mile and continue for 1.2 miles. Turn right at the sign for the College Conservation Area at the bottom of a hill, then fork right and park at the tennis courts.

To reach the Weston Reservoir area, turn left off Rte. 20 at the traffic signal on School St. Continue straight for 0.7 miles, then bear right on Ash St. The parking area is less than a half-mile ahead.

PUBLIC TRANSPORTATION:

The Fitchburg Line stops at Kendall Green in Weston, a few miles from the center of town. Leaving the station, turn right on Church St. and continue for 1.1 miles to Boston Post Rd. at the center of town. To reach the College Conservation Area, turn right on Boston Post Rd. and then right on Concord Rd. To reach the Weston Reservoir trailhead, continue across Boston Post Rd. and Rte. 20 on School St., then bear right on Ash St.

BIKE SHOPS:

Frank's Spoke 'n Wheel, 887 Main St. (Rte. 20), Waltham, Tel. (781) 894-2768

Harris Cyclery, 1355 Washington St. (Rte. 16), West Newton, Tel. (617) 244-1040

Lincoln Guide Service, 152 Lincoln Rd., Lincoln, Tel. (781) 259-9204

St. Moritz Sports, 475 Washington St. (Rte. 16), Wellesley, Tel. (781) 235-6669

ADDITIONAL INFORMATION:

Weston Forest and Trail Association, Weston Town Hall, P.O. Box 378, Weston, MA 02193

17
Callahan State Park
Framingham

Positioned between the populations of Framingham and Marlborough, Callahan State Park is a beloved oasis. The park lies only a few minutes from the hustle of both Rte. 9 and Rte. 20 but harbors nearly 15 miles of trails with a level of peace and quiet usually reserved for more remote areas. Its great variety of trails offers something for every mountain biker, from wide and smooth to narrow and bumpy.

BACKGROUND:

Together with neighboring watershed properties and Sudbury Valley Trustees conservation lands, Callahan State Park preserves a surprisingly natural and pastoral corner of suburbia. With the state's relatively recent purchase of the northern half of the park, Callahan now totals 819 acres of public land.

Hunting and the use of motorized vehicles are not permitted. The park remains in a relatively undeveloped state with no staff or facilities on site but its trails are typically alive with local residents out for their daily exercise.

TRAIL POLICIES:

Callahan is managed by the staff at Cochituate State Park, who advise mountain bikers to expect plenty of foot traffic on the trails. The park's proximity to population makes it a popular place for runners, dogwalkers, and those out for a short stroll so ride cautiously and be ready to yield trail. Remember to avoid startling others by making your presence known at a safe distance.

The park's boundaries form a long, thin patchwork of acreage and segments of several trails lie on private lands. A few display *No Trespassing* signs while certain others are posted as being off limits only to bicycling. Please respect the landowner's requests. Currently all of the park's trails are open to mountain biking but check for trailhead notices before you ride.

Signs display trail names at some points but the high density of intersections can be confusing so pay careful attention to the map.

The park's trails lie in two separate groups, each with a trailhead parking lot to provide access. **North Entrance**, on the Marlborough side, serves mostly single-tracks in a challenging area for mountain biking and **South Entrance**, on the more popular Framingham side, serves smoother, flatter, wider trails for easy and intermediate riding. Both sides are connected by trails through private conservation land owned by the Sudbury Valley Trustees.

Starting at South Entrance, **Moore Road** welcomes bicyclists with a smooth, gravelly surface. After crossing a long earthen dam built for flood control, it stretches across three fields and then continues into the woods intersecting other trails along the way. In the last of the fields look to the right for Eagle Pond, a good picnicking spot.

A short distance beyond the pond look for **Pinecone Path** which forks left at the edge of the woods and follows the park's boundary westward on a gentle uphill, tracing the backyards of abutting residences. Exposed tree roots make some parts a bumpy ride before it ends near Fox Hill Rd.

Rocky Road is a much smoother trail than its name implies and provides an easy route northward from the end of Pinecone Path. After 0.8 miles it narrows and enters private conservation land owned by the Sudbury Valley Trustees where bicycling is not permitted. To continue on this property cyclists must walk their bikes for 2 tenths of a mile to more state park acreage at the **Red Tail Trail**.

Alternatively, turn right on **Fox Hunt Trail** to return to the trailhead. A mostly downhill run, Fox Hunt encounters some difficulty after crossing Juniper Lane where the slope

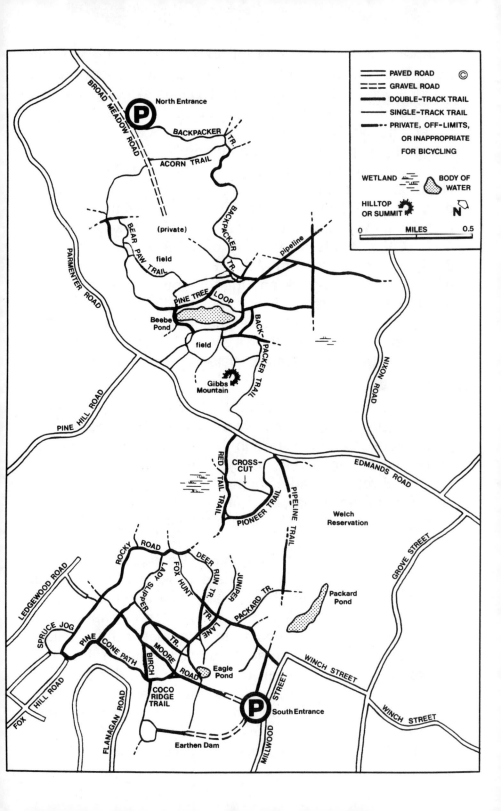

steepens and erosion has left loose rocks. Beyond this point the trail flattens, turns right and crosses a large wooden bridge, then climbs a gentle slope along an old road that heads to Millwood St. Just before it reaches the pavement, look for a right turn that crosses a large field and returns to the parking lot in a quarter-mile.

Combining Moore Road, Pinecone Path, Rocky Road, and Fox Hunt Trail makes a 2.5-mile loop of mostly easy riding. Tree roots, rocks, and perhaps some wet spots hamper a few places but they can easily be walked.

Other trails offer easy options within this loop. **Juniper Lane** rises from Moore Road to the top of a small hill, first as double-track and then narrowing to single-track, and reaches an area of juniper bushes that once thrived in the open sunlight of a hillside pasture but are now shaded by forest. As it crests the hill the trail enters the Sudbury Valley Trustees' land where bicycles must be walked.

SINGLE-TRACKS:

The hillier northern part of the park holds most of the single-tracks and gets less overall use. Blue, triangular tree tags mark some of the trails in this area and bear a symbol of the trail's name, while many of the unmarked trails are peripheral routes dead-ending at private property. Visitors should note that a parcel of private property exists at the end of Broadmeadow Rd. in the center of this part of the park.

The **Backpacker Trail**, the park's longest route, runs for 1.5 miles to Edmands Rd. where it links the Red Tail Trail and the park's southern half. Marked by tree tags bearing the image of a hiker, it begins at the North Entrance and heads uphill on a rocky course then merges with the milder **Acorn Trail** and continues over mellower terrain. The Backpacker turns right on the treeless corridor of a gas pipeline, drops on a steep hill, then turns left at the bottom and reenters the woods on a double-track. It turns through several more intersections before finishing with a nice section of single-track on a side hill of Gibbs Mountain.

126

The **Pine Tree Loop** intersects the Backpacker Trail at the bottom of the pipeline hill and circles Beebe Pond with a scenic ride on both single- and double-tracks. Look for the **Bear Paw Trail**, marked by tree tags bearing a claw print, to return to the North Entrance trailhead with some intermediate-level single-track. It climbs from the pond at an old chimney, flattens in a large field, then descends through the woods to Broadmeadow Rd. near the parking lot. Combining the Backpacker, Pine Tree, and Bear Paw trails makes an intermediate, 2.7-mile ride.

DRIVING DIRECTIONS:

To reach the south entrance from I-90, take Exit 12 and follow Rte. 9 east for 2 miles. Exit at signs for Main St. and Edgell Rd., then turn left on Main St. and continue for 0.2 miles. Turn left on Vernon St., then right on Grove St., drive for 2 miles and turn left on Winch St. After the road turns hard left it becomes Millwood St. and the parking lot is 0.2 miles ahead on the right.

To reach the north entrance from I-495 take Exit 24A for Rte. 20 east. After 4 miles turn right on Farm Rd., then turn left on Broadmeadow St. Continue straight on Broadmeadow and the parking lot is 0.8 miles ahead on the left.

BIKE SHOPS:

Frank's Spoke 'n Wheel, 1164 Worcester Rd. (Rte. 9 eastbound), Framingham, Tel. (508) 872-8590

Landry's Cycling & Fitness, 303 Worcester Rd. (Rte. 9 westbound), Framingham, Tel. (508) 875-5158

Ski Market, 686 Worcester Rd. (Rte. 9 eastbound), Framingham, Tel. (508) 875-5253

Yankee Pedaler, 141 Main St., Hudson, Tel. (978) 568-9070

ADDITIONAL INFORMATION:

Callahan State Park, c/o Cochituate State Park, 93 Commonwealth Rd., Cochituate, MA 01778, (508) 653-9641

Sudbury Valley Trustees, P.O. Box 7, Wayland, MA 01778, Tel. (508) 443-6300

18
Hopkinton State Park
Hopkinton

Hopkinton State Park's huge capacity is geared toward serving the thousands of visitors who arrive each summer eager to swim at its broad beaches and relax in the shade of its trees, but a small collection of trails lurking in the woods nearby satisfies mountain bikers with year-round fun. Not the place for long tours, Hopkinton State Park is suited for shorter rides.

BACKGROUND:

The park's origin lies with its centerpiece, a 185-acre reservoir which was built between 1891 and 1894 as a water source for Boston. After construction of the Quabbin Reservoir in central Massachusetts left the Hopkinton no longer needed for water supply, the property was transferred to the Department of Environmental Management and developed as a recreational area complete with picnic facilities, two swimming beaches, playing fields, and an impressive fleet of parking lots.

These amenities lie in the area north of the reservoir where a network of paved roads serves the masses of visitors in summer. A small entrance fee is charged at the point of entry. Toilets are available during the warm season and life guards supervise the beaches from Memorial Day through Labor Day.

TRAIL POLICIES:

All trails are open for mountain biking at the time of publication. Riders should use extra caution, however, on trails in the area of the reservoir and parking lots since they are heavily traveled by walkers, especially in summer. Pedal at a safe speed, announce your presence early to avoid startling anyone, and be willing to yield trail. The park's outlying paths are typically abandoned and offer a

129

much more solitary experience.

ORIENTATION:

The high density of trails, roads, and parking lots north of the reservoir can be confusing. Fortunately, each parking lot is identified by a letter painted on a yellow post near its entrance which is displayed on the map. Trails in this small area are named and illustrated in detail on the park's trail map which is available at the contact station.

DOUBLE-TRACKS:

Close to the reservoir, a number of smooth double-tracks lead beachgoers from the parking lots downhill to the beach areas. Although the surfaces are free of much trouble, many of the routes have slopes that will require extra energy. The Hardwood Trail makes a mostly smooth, steady descent that begins near parking lot F and arrives at the reservoir near lot J. Rocky Road is an intermediate ride with some loose rocks on the surface as it drops on a slope heading toward the water from parking lot A. The Quarry Trail makes this same elevation change from parking lot E with a smoother, pebbly surface. The **Foxtrot Trail** is an intermediate ride from the contact station through a scattering of exposed rocks and encounters a difficult section of single-track at its southern terminus.

Farther afield, the **Duck Pond Trail** provides 1.3 miles of riding to the quiet scenery at Duck Pond, with mostly easy conditions but one intermediate section. The trail begins behind the park headquarters complex with a smooth and firm surface. After crossing Indian Brook the trail rises on a few moderate slopes, intersects another double-track at the half-mile mark, and continues into an area of intermediate conditions where rocks bulge from the ground. Easy riding returns after a short distance but the trail ends at private property shortly after it passes the lily pads of Duck Pond. A single-track with intermediate conditions continues the ride for another half-mile around the northern shore of the pond to Saddle Hill Rd.

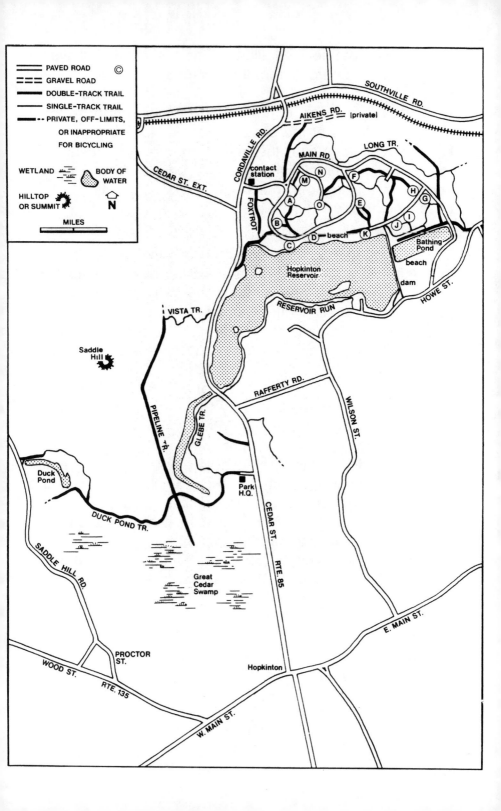

The **Pipeline Trail** allows a more strenuous diversion to this trip. It emerges from the darkness and mud of Great Cedar Swamp heading northward on the straight-line course of a utility corridor, climbing and descending several strenuous slopes at the base of Saddle Hill along the way. Eroded conditions earn the trail an intermediate rating. At the trail's high point, just before it leaves state property, riders can turn right on the single-track Vista Trail which is described below.

SINGLE-TRACKS:

The park has a fun collection of short single-tracks in the main use area near the reservoir but bikers should plan on slow speeds since walkers frequent these narrow pathways, especially in the warm season. The trails weave through the trees on tight courses that have mostly smooth treadways defined by overgrowing bushes, and descend as they approach the water. The Caesar Trail is a rockier option as it slips through an area of boulders and ledge for an intermediate ride. Down by the water, the Arborvitae Trail follows an easy and flat stretch of shoreline in the cool shade of arborvitae trees west of parking lot C.

Outside of this area, single-tracks run for greater distances. Look for the start of the 1.5-mile **Long Trail** just uphill from the contact station on Main Road. A mostly intermediate ride with a few difficult sections, it starts with a descent along an old wagon road, turns right and climbs through a stone wall, then continues with a downward coast for another quarter-mile through pretty forest and more stone walls. It climbs back to the side of Main Road with a rocky section, then continues with more rough areas and a series of ups and downs for the next 0.6 miles to another old wagon road. Crossing it, Long Trail runs for another third of a mile with easy riding on flat terrain and a smooth treadway before ending at Main Road near the Bathing Pond.

Reservoir Run is a recommended, mile-long trip along the southern shoreline of Hopkinton Reservoir. It starts on Howe St. a short distance from the dam and has easy riding conditions on relatively flat and smooth ground for the first half-mile. The second half-mile has intermediate conditions with several short, steep hills to climb and an abundance of tree roots to survive. Note that this trail follows a narrow strip of state park land and that intersecting paths lead to private property.

Two single-tracks west of Rte. 85 are worth a try. The **Vista Trail**, undeserving of its name, is nevertheless an excellent downhill ride from the Pipeline Trail to the reservoir with a swerving, half-mile course through the trees. Occasional rocks provide obstacles on an otherwise smooth surface. The **Glebe Trail** starts at a bridge nearby with flat conditions at the edge of a long, slender pond until it turns toward the headquarters complex and struggles through several small hills.

DRIVING DIRECTIONS:

From I-495 take Exit 21A for West Main St. Continue for 1.5 miles (joining Rte. 135 east along the way), then turn left (north) on Rte. 85 at a traffic signal. The park's main entrance is 2.3 miles ahead on the right.

BIKE SHOPS:

Biicycle Barn, 123 Boston Tpk. (Rte 9 westbound), Westboro, Tel. (508) 366-1770

Frank's Spoke 'n Wheel, 1164 Worcester Rd. (Rte. 9 eastbound, Framinham, Tel. (508) 872-8590

Landry's Cycling & Fitness, 303 Worcester Rd. (Rte. 9 westbound), Framingham, Tel. (508) 875-5158

Milford Bicycle, 71 E. Main St. (Rte 16), Milford, Tel. (508) 473-7955

Ski Market, 686 Worcester Rd. (Rte. 9 eastbound), Framingham, Tel. (508) 875-5253

Specialty Ski & Bike, 267 Hartford Ave. (Rte. 126), Bellingham, Tel. (508) 966-5000

Trek Stop, 156 Main St. (Rte. 122A), Grafton, Tel. (508) 839-9199

ADDITIONAL INFORMATION:

Hopkinton State Park, 71 Cedar St., Hopkinton, MA 01748, Tel. (508) 435-4303

19
Upton State Forest
Upton

Located near the intersection of interstates 495 and 90, these hilly 2,660 acres hold a surprising 25 miles of mountain biking trails that include old forest roads and a fresh crop of single-tracks. Relatively few other visitors find their way to this state forest so fat tire tracks abound.

BACKGROUND:

Upton State Forest was established in the early 1930's and, like many other large, state-owned properties, served as a camp for the Civilian Conservation Corps during the Great Depression. The camp's occupants built the buildings that comprise Forest Headquarters as well as many of the roads and trails that visitors use today. The state forest has no developed facilities other than its trails.

TRAIL POLICIES:

The stable near the trailhead is home to several horses that the staff uses to patrol the area so be ready to meet them on the trails. Mountain biking is permitted on all trails at Upton State Forest but officials ask riders to control their bikes, avoid skidding, and avoid startling horses and hikers by announcing their presence at a safe distance. Note that the property forms a patchwork of acreage and that many peripheral trails stray onto private property. The area is open from sunrise to sunset.

ORIENTATION:

The woods roads that spread southward from the trailhead have riding conditions that range from easy to difficult, while the single-track options hold intermediate and difficult riding. Major points of reference for locating your position include Westboro Rd. running along the western side of the forest and the treeless corridors of two utility lines near the southern boundary.

Almost all trails are named and marked with wooden signs. Several trails are freshly cut and could be faint in places until the treadway becomes established so watch for the blue tree tags that mark their courses.

DOUBLE-TRACKS:

Beginning at the trailhead parking lot, **Park Road** is the main route through the forest and leads past the metal gate on a 2.3-mile, southerly course to Hopkinton Rd. over some of the forest's biggest hills. Its surface is broad and gravelly but many of the slopes have loose rocks that deserve careful attention, especially on the downhills. Park Road forks right at the first intersection and climbs for an arduous half-mile before cresting the hill and descending swiftly to a major intersection with **Dean Pond Road** at the 1.2-mile mark. It continues over gentler terrain for another mile to a metal gate at the forest's southern boundary where several sets of powerlines buzz overhead a short distance from Hopkinton Rd.

Loop Road forks left from Park Road near the parking lot and offers milder hills. It starts with a smaller climb and continues with a more manageable descent but loose rocks make its slopes equally tricky and a few sandy patches can mire bicycle tires. Loop Road finishes with an easy approach to **Dean Pond**, a scenic spot for a picnic or rest. A dam on the opposite shore contains the water and originates from the 1790's when it powered a small sawmill. Combining Park Road, Dean Pond Road, and Loop Road forms an intermediate, 3-mile ride that is easiest in the counter-clockwise direction.

Trails intersecting this loop hold mostly intermediate and difficult conditions. **Whitehall Road** is the easiest option, branching at the base of a hill and running over flat terrain for less than a mile to a state forest boundary marker. Nearby **Bridge Road** is a bumpy ride from tree roots of surrounding pines. It begins with a flat half-mile and then turns right at an intersection and rises on a gentle grade, crosses the open corridor of a gas pipeline, and ends on

136

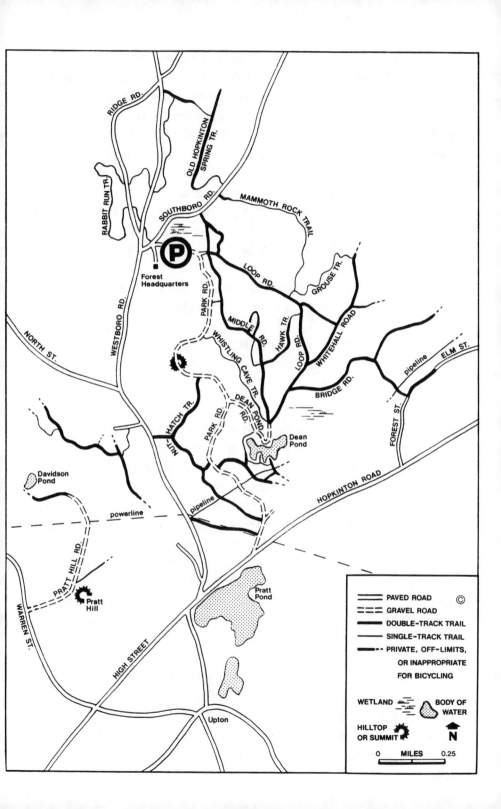

Elm St. in Hopkinton which becomes Forest St. in Upton.

Middle Road dates from the mid-1700's when it served a homestead. Following stone walls for much of the way, the old road rises from Dean Pond with an eroded surface for the first quarter-mile, then rises more gradually to the top of a small hill and descends. After crossing a small streambed on the opposite side of the hill, the trail narrows and takes a rolling course to Loop Road near the parking lot. It is intermediate riding for most of its 1.1-mile distance. The adjoining **Hawk Trail** climbs to the high point on Middle Road from Whitehall Road with a similar ride of exposed rocks and moderate slopes.

Difficult riding awaits on the mile-long **Nuthatch Trail** where some challenging hills and eroded surfaces test both strength and skill. Two trails provide bail-out points along the way: one returns to Park Road near Dean Pond and the other connects the pavement of Westboro Rd. about a mile from the parking lot.

SINGLE-TRACKS:

The half-mile-long **Whistling Cave Trail** explores some interesting sites near the center of the state forest. Marked by blue tree tags, the path is hindered by rocks, logs, stone walls, and stream beds and is suited only for the most ambitious cyclists. Starting at the highest endpoint near the top of the hill on Park Road, the trail passes an open ledge with a view of the horizon and then drops over the edge on a steep slope that will require walking. It continues through the valley below this ledge, climbs the opposite side, and finishes with another downhill near the intersection of Middle and Loop roads. Look for Whistling Cave, an overhanging boulder, near the top of the last downhill.

A collection of new single-tracks climbs the hills at the northern end of the forest. The **Rabbit Run Trail** begins across **Southboro Road** from the forest's entrance driveway and makes a loop on the hillside above Ridge Rd. following some of the stone walls that mark the property

138

boundary. The hills are rideable and conditions are generally intermediate. After a downhill ride to Westboro Rd. where it intersects a few overgrown snowmobile routes, the trail runs north alongside the street for a half-mile and turns east to climb over a small hill. It then joins a segment of the **Hopkinton Spring Trail**, an old wagon track lined with stone walls, and reverts to single-track before returning to Southboro Rd. with an abrupt drop.

Look for the **Mammoth Rock Trail** beginning almost directly across the street from this point. Linking the main trail network along a corridor of state forest land, this path is a mostly intermediate ride from its plentiful tree stumps, wet spots, and hills. It is named for the huge granite outcropping visible beside the trail near the southern endpoint. The adjoining **Grouse Trail** is a more difficult trip that winds up and down hills where erosion has exposed many rocks and roots. Its final drop to Whitehall Road is especially steep.

DRIVING DIRECTIONS:

From I-495 take Exit 21B and follow Rte. 135 west toward Upton for 3.5 miles. Turn right on Westboro Rd. opposite Pratt Pond and continue for 2 miles to the state forest sign on the right. Turn right on Southboro Rd., then right on a gravel road that is the state forest's entrance.

BIKE SHOPS:

Milford Bicycle, 71 E. Main St. (Rte 16), Milford, Tel. (508) 473-7955

Specialty Ski & Bike, 267 Hartford Ave. (Rte. 126), Bellingham, Tel. (508) 966-5000

Trek Stop, 156 Main St. (Rte. 122A), Grafton, Tel. (508) 839-9199

ADDITIONAL INFORMATION:

Upton State Forest, 205 Westboro Rd., Upton, MA 01568, Tel. (508) 529-6923

20
Blackstone River & Canal
Heritage State Park
Uxbridge

Together with the public land at neighboring West Hill Dam, this park offers interesting historical relics, beautiful natural scenery, and 10 miles of trails that range from easy to difficult. In summer, bring a swimsuit and/or a picnic and plan to stay a while.

BACKGROUND:

The Blackstone River had been described as one of the hardest working rivers in the country in the late 1700's and early 1800's when it powered dozens of small mills that produced flour, boards, and iron goods. It was also home to America's first water-powered textile factory. Between the years 1828 and 1848 the river supported a 45-mile canal that linked Worcester and Providence with a transportation source for exporting local products and importing foreign goods from around the world.

A railroad eventually killed the canal's business but a 3.5-mile stretch of the waterway is preserved in this heritage state park and brought back to life with an interpretive brochure and visitor center exhibits. Bikers, hikers, canoeists, and other exercisers now draw strength from the Blackstone as they travel its course and admire the views.

TRAIL POLICIES:

Mountain biking is permitted on all trails. Bicyclists should note, however, that hikers are the predominant user group at both Blackstone and West Hill Dam, especially on weekends. Many of the park's trails are narrow so travel at an appropriate speed and be ready to yield. Dogs must be leashed.

ORIENTATION:

The park's natural features provide helpful points of

reference when exploring for the first time. At Blackstone, the river and canal are the backbone to the property and, together with surrounding hills and intersecting roads, guide the trails along a north-south corridor. Numbered historical sites located along the canal are described in an interpretive brochure (available at the visitor center) that can also help determine your location. At West Hill Dam, the trail system forms a simple loop around a piece of the West River with roads crossing at three points. Maps and signs are posted to help guide visitors.

DOUBLE-TRACKS:

Starting from the Stanley Woolen Mill, the park's southernmost point, the **Blackstone Canal Towpath** heads northward beside the waterway, now an idle pool in the shade of surrounding trees. Towpaths, built on the banks along the entire length of the canal, were used by horses to pull loaded boats through the water. Today tree roots ripple the towpath's surface in a few places but it is an otherwise flat, smooth and easy ride.

A mile from the mill is a wooden bridge across the canal leading to the **visitor center**, once a barn of Riverbend Farm. When it is open, the staffed building offers toilet facilities, drinking water, and information.

Continuing north, the towpath runs for another quarter-mile to Hartford Ave., where two magnificent stone arches bridge the river and canal. Cross the pavement and look for the **Goat Hill Trail** heading across a small field and into the woods at a trailhead sign. Rocks and roots are more plentiful on this trail but they are sporadic and avoidable so the riding is intermediate, even when the treadway narrows to single-track near the midsection. Goat Hill Trail follows a shelf of land above the open wetland known as Rice City Pond.

Site 5 on the map marks the Goat Hill Lock, one of many points that joined sections of the canal that were at different elevations. Here boats could either ascend or descend in elevation by the emptying or filling of water

142

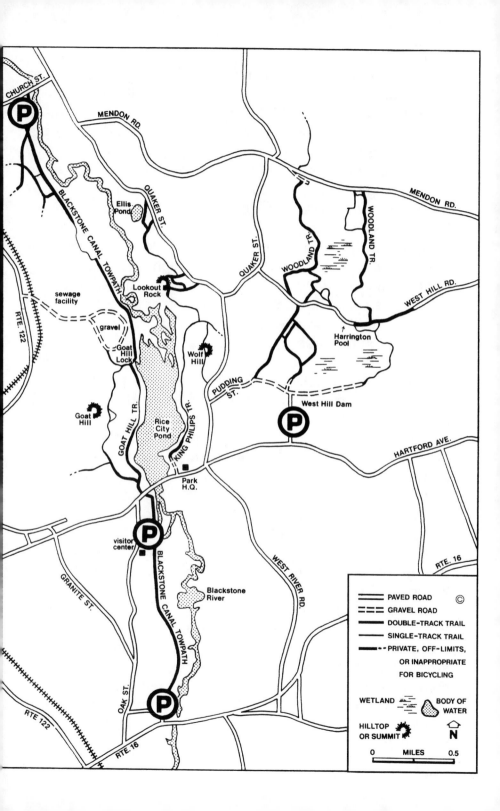

inside the lock.

Plummer's Trail, named for a local merchant during the canal's boom years, runs along a towpath for 1.8 miles from the lock to Church St. The trail is bumpy with more tree roots and narrows to single-track for a brief distance but remains a generally easy ride.

The land surrounding nearby **West Hill Dam** harbors a swimming beach, picnic area, and about 5 miles of trails in a flood control area managed by the U.S. Army Corps of Engineers. Constructed in the late 1950's, this dam is designed to hold water only in times of flooding to prevent damage downstream and is usually high and dry. During periods of river flooding, do not expect to be able to use these trails since they could be under water.

Marked in orange, the **Woodland Trail** is a 3.6-mile loop through the area with mostly easy riding, although one avoidable section has intermediate conditions. Following the loop in the clockwise direction from the parking lot off Hartford Ave., ride up the paved access road, turn left, and pass through a yellow gate on a gravel road that travels along a low extension of the huge, earthen dam. Turn right after a quarter-mile and continue for a half-mile on an old farm road that has a smooth surface of processed stone, then cross West Hill Rd. at a small parking lot and continue northward into the woods. The next mile of trail to Mendon St. is mostly flat with tree roots creating a few bumps.

Ride out to Mendon St., turn right, and follow the pavement across the river. The orange dots of the Woodland Trail reenter the woods after a quarter-mile on the right and run southward for almost a mile back to West Hill Rd. with mostly easy rolling. A few spots are rough but they are short-lived and easily walked. The remaining half-mile single-track to the dam is intermediate riding from a combination of roots, rocks, and slopes but can be avoided by turning right on West Hill Rd. and returning on the trail's first leg. The picnic area and beach at the river's Harrington Pool makes a nice rest stop at the center of this loop.

Most of the single-track options are at Blackstone. The path that loops to the top of **Goat Hill** is difficult to ride but manageable for experts who can handle steep slopes and maneuver around plentiful rocks. An open ledge near the top allows a slight view. The trail is most rideable from the south where the slope is a bit more gradual.

Across the river, the **King Philips Trail** provides another difficult ride for over a mile to one of the park's most spectacular points. It starts at Park Headquarters with a broad, smooth surface but narrows when it enters the woods and struggles with trees and roots, slipping past a wetland at the foot of a hill. At the end climb atop **Lookout Rock** for a great view over the Blackstone Valley. Be aware that this is a popular destination for hikers and that the surrounding trails will require good trail manners. For a less-traveled alternative, try the single-track that climbs over **Wolf Hill**.

DRIVING DIRECTIONS:

From I-495, take Exit 20 if southbound (for Rte. 85 south) or Exit 19 if northbound (for Rte. 109 west) and follow signs to Rte. 16. To reach the park's southern endpoint, take Rte. 16 west for 8 miles from the intersection of Route 85, then turn right on Cross St. The parking lot is ahead on the right. For the visitor center, continue on Rte. 16 to Oak St., turn right, and find the parking lot on the right after a mile. For West Hill Dam, drive for 4.5 miles west on Rte. 16 (from Rte. 85), turn right on Hartford Ave., and the dam's access road is 2.3 miles ahead on the right.

BIKE SHOPS:

Blackstone Canal Bicycles, 2 S. Main St. (Rte. 122), Uxbridge, Tel. (508) 278-3080

Milford Bicycle, 71 E. Main St. (Rte16), Milford, Tel. (508) 473-7955

Specialty Ski & Bike, 267 Hartford Ave. (Rte. 126), Bellingham, Tel. (508) 966-5000

ADDITIONAL INFORMATION:

Blackstone River & Canal Heritage State Park, 287 Oak St., Uxbridge, MA 01569, Tel. (508) 278-7604

West Hill Dam Project Office, RR#2, Box 45E-1, Uxbridge, MA 01569-9608, Tel. (508) 278-2511

21
Douglas State Forest
Douglas

The diversity of trails at Douglas State Forest offers something for everyone. Mountain bikers can choose between unpaved rail-trails, gravel fire roads, bumpy double-tracks, rock-infested hiking trails, and a challenging set of former motorcycle paths.

BACKGROUND:

George Washington described his route through what is now Douglas State Forest as an *"intolerable, bad road and a poor, uncultivated country."* For years since that time this boulder-strewn landscape attracted only workers for jobs such as brickmaking, ice cutting, and granite quarrying until its wild and natural qualities were recognized by the state in 1934, when the forest was established. The initial purchase of 1,245 acres served a camp for the Civilian Conservation Corps during the Great Depression when the beach, trails, and fire roads were created. Today Wallum Lake is the forest's main attraction for summer visitors but the remaining 5,000 acres of woodlands are a recreational haven for others as well.

Given its vast acreage and remote location Douglas is a popular place for hunting during deer season in the late fall. Mountain biking is discouraged at this time, except on Sundays when hunting is prohibited by state law.

TRAIL POLICIES:

Mountain bikers are advised not to ride the single-track sections of the Coffeehouse Loop and Cedar Swamp Trail which are intended to be interpretive nature paths for walkers. All other trails are open for riding.

A fee is charged for parking at Wallum Beach at the southern end of the forest during the warm season when hundreds of people arrive to swim and picnic, so park at either of the two northern lots at this time of year unless you plan to use the beach. The forest's staff requests that bikes be walked through crowded areas and over lawns.

ORIENTATION:

Douglas State Forest has a long, thin shape that extends in the north-south direction. The property is divided by two public roads, Rte. 16 and Southwest Main St., running east-west and is bordered on the eastern side by several more, providing helpful features for orientation. Trail signs are scarce but first-time visitors will find that the numbered gates, installed to block vehicle entry at trail/road intersections, are a useful aid in identifying a location. These gate numbers appear on the accompanying map.

GRAVEL ROADS:

The 3-mile **Ridge Trail** offers one of the forest's easiest surfaces for pedaling. Well-drained and smooth, this gravel road runs between the parking lot on Wallis St. and Northwest Main St. and encounters several hills along the way, with a significant climb and descent located near the crossing of Coopertown Brook at the western reach of Wallis Reservoir. Combining the Ridge Trail with the pavement of adjoining roads completes a 4.7-mile loop.

To the south, the **Streeter Trail** is another obstacle-free route spanning the 1.6-mile distance between gate 21 on Wallum Pond Rd. and gate 15 on Southwest Main St. It too has a few hill climbs but the route holds peaceful forest scenery and provides an important linkage between the north and south halves of the forest.

DOUBLE-TRACKS:

The double-tracks at Douglas come in all varieties, from easy to difficult. Among the flattest is the **Southern New England Trunkline Trail**, an unpaved rail-trail following a straight route from Franklin, MA to Willimantic, CT. With the rails and ties removed, wooden bridges spanning streams, and a gravel surface, the grade is ideal for biking and enjoys especially good scenery in a

148

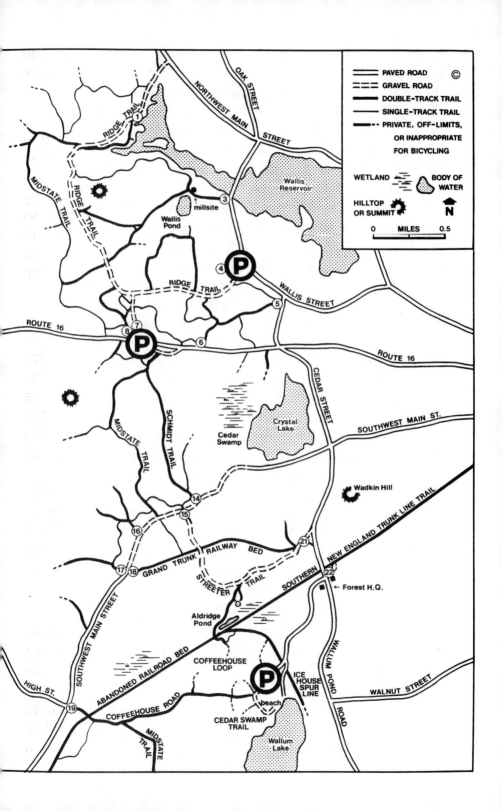

combination of woods and open wetlands. Two easy routes access the Trunk Line Trail with the most direct being a gravel road at gate 22 beside the Fire Control building on Wallum Pond Rd. Another is the **Ice House Spur Line**, a former railroad that was built to transport ice cut at Wallum Pond, connecting the beach access road a half-mile from the trail. Note that the double-track linking the Streeter Trail at Aldridge Pond is a bumpy ride over exposed rocks.

A third rail-trail, the **Grand Trunk Railway Bed**, lies nearby. Its numerous hill-cuts and massive, earthen causeways create a level route through rolling terrain but tree roots ripple the surface at several points. Although it consumed a great amount of work, this railroad was never completed because the project's financial backer, Charles Hays, was killed with the sinking of the *Titanic* in 1912.

The 1.2-mile **Schmidt Trail** is another easy ride but it follows a more natural course of hills and turns through a vast oak forest. Recently improved, this smooth trail is lined with the rocks that were extracted from its surface. Two high points mark the midsection.

The unnamed double-tracks north of Rte. 16 have easy and intermediate conditions. A scattering of exposed rocks and roots disrupt the surfaces of these trails and rolling terrain adds life to the riding.

Paralleling the Schmidt Trail, one of the state forest's most difficult double-tracks is a segment of the **Midstate Trail** where an abundance of huge rocks hinders wheels of any kind. Another is **Coffeehouse Road**, an old wagon track that struggles over rocks, water bars, and a few wet spots for 1.5 miles between Wallum Lake and gate 19 on Southwest Main St. Stone walls line much of this route, named for a nearby stage coach stop of earlier times.

SINGLE-TRACKS:

The single-tracks have difficult, rocky conditions and many are extremely technical and will require some walking. Originally made by off-road motorcycles, most lie north of Rte. 16 although a string of narrow paths offers mountain bikers a challenging ride alongside Southwest Main St between gates 14 and 17. At the northern tip of the forest several single-tracks combine with the Ridge Trail to form a difficult, 2-mile loop through a seldom-traveled area of hills, logs, and overgrowing bushes. The trail along the southern shore of Wallis Reservoir, roughened by rocks, roots, and a steep hill, should be ridden in the west-to-east (more downhill) direction.

The Midstate Trail, a yellow-blazed trail through Douglas State Forest that extends from Rhode Island to New Hampshire, is a rugged course for biking. Many sections are too rocky to ride so be prepared for carries.

DRIVING DIRECTIONS:

From I-495 take Exit 19 (if northbound) or Exit 20 (if southbound) and follow signs for Rte. 16 west through Milford, Hopedale, Mendon, Uxbridge, and Douglas. After 17 miles, Rte. 16 turns right at an intersection with Rte. 96. For the Wallis St. parking lot, continue on Rte. 16 for another 1.4 miles, turn right on Cedar St., left on Wallis St., and look for the lot on the left. For the Rte. 16 parking lot, continue for another mile beyond Cedar St. on Rte. 16. The lot is on the left side.

BIKE SHOPS:

Barney's Bicycle, 165 Chandler St. (Rte. 122), Worcester, Tel. (508) 757-3754

Bicycle Alley, 1067 Main St., Worcester, Tel. (508) 752-2230

Blackstone Canal Bicycles, 2 S. Main St. (Rte. 122), Uxbridge, Tel. (508) 278-3080

Fritz's Bicycle Shop, 328 W. Boylston St., Worcester, Tel. (508) 853-1799

Goatwheels Bicycle Shop, 30 Oxford Ave., Dudley, Tel. (508) 949-2012

Milford Bicycle, 71 East Main St. (Rte. 16), Milford, Tel. (508) 473-7955

O'Neil's Bicycle Shop, 1094 Main St., Worcester, Tel. (800) 638-6344

Trek Stop, 156 Main St., Grafton, Tel. (508) 839-9199

ADDITIONAL INFORMATION:

Douglas State Forest, 108 Wallum Lake Rd., Douglas, MA 01516, Tel. (508) 476-7872

22
Franklin State Forest
Franklin

Lacking even a trailhead parking lot, Franklin State Forest is a little-known tract of land that is great for mountain biking. About 15 miles of intermediate-level trails include both wagon roads and winding motorcycle paths that are much less hilly and rocky than those at neighboring state properties.

BACKGROUND:

The state began acquiring land here in the 1930's and the property hosted a Civilian Conservation Corps camp for a brief period during the Great Depression. Once farmland, the acreage has reverted to forest and the old wagon roads that once divided the fields are now useful recreational trails in the shade of deep woods. Several of these routes officially remain town roads that are no longer maintained for regular travel.

Except for its trails, the forest is undeveloped and no facilities or staff are present. Mountain biking is one of the most common activities but hiking, horseback riding, off-road motorcycling, and hunting are also permitted.

TRAIL POLICIES:

Franklin State Forest is managed by the staff at F. Gilbert Hills State Forest in Foxborough. Given the area's history of motorcycle usage, trail erosion is a noticeable problem so do your best to minimize impact. Avoid skidding, stay on the trail's treadway to prevent any widening of the surface, and never ride when conditions are wet.

Since the forest has no trailhead parking lot, visitors are advised to park along the side of Forge Hill Rd. leaving space for other vehicles to pass. Do not block the gate at the end of the pavement since work vehicles always need access to the road.

The trails are not marked with signs and most routes do not have names. The double-tracks, which are old farm roads, cross the forest at various points and surround the single-tracks, which are a confusing tangle of motorcycle paths. Since the single-tracks are not marked, pay careful attention to the map at each intersection that you encounter.

Most of the trails lie on the gradual slopes of the west, south, and east sides of Forge Hill, a high point which provides a general sense of direction. Since the trailhead is at the top, remember that your return will require an uphill ride.

Continuing past the gate at the end of **Forge Hill Road**, the surface changes from pavement to eroded trail as riders descend the western slope. Rocks and ruts make this brief section a tricky ride. Flattening at the bottom, the trail reaches a four-way intersection at Spring Street and then resumes its downward course for another half-mile before leaving the state forest.

Spring Street is one of the town's oldest roads and appears on the area's earliest maps. Although it is still a public way, the road has been unmaintained for years and is merely a trail now, spanning the 2.5-mile distance from Rte. 140 in the north to Washington St. in the south with intermediate riding conditions. Its midsection lies within the state forest boundaries but each end is bordered by private lands so keep to the trail in those areas. North of Forge Hill Road, Spring Street descends at a moderate grade for three quarters of a mile to Rte. 140. To the south it follows a stone wall past several intersecting single-tracks and descends the southern slope of Forge Hill, flattening after a half-mile at the edge of a wetland. A few wet spots slow the pedaling at this point but the trail soon regains high ground, emerges in a farm field, and drops on a short slope past several homes to Washington St.

Near this southern terminus look for the **Southern**

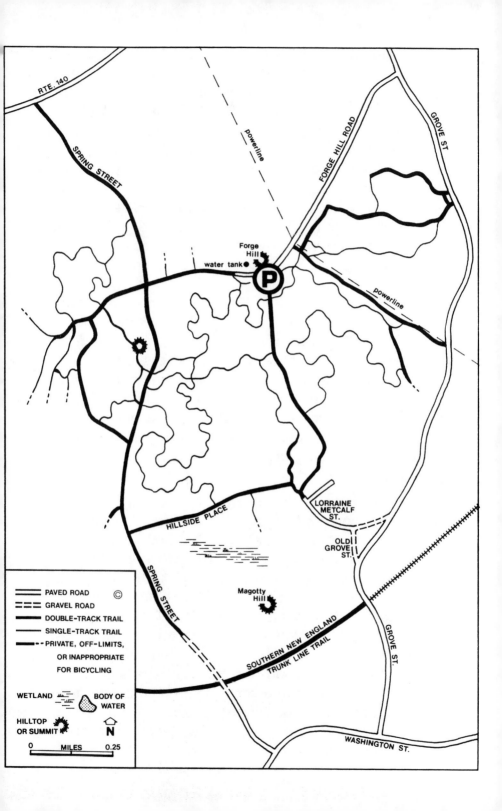

RTE. 140

SPRING STREET

FORGE HILL ROAD

GROVE ST.

powerline

Forge Hill

water tank

P

powerline

LORRAINE METCALF ST.

HILLSIDE PLACE

OLD GROVE ST.

SPRING STREET

Magotty Hill

SOUTHERN NEW ENGLAND TRUNK LINE TRAIL

GROVE ST.

WASHINGTON ST.

PAVED ROAD ©
GRAVEL ROAD
DOUBLE-TRACK TRAIL
SINGLE-TRACK TRAIL
PRIVATE, OFF-LIMITS,
OR INAPPROPRIATE
FOR BICYCLING

WETLAND   BODY OF
               WATER

HILLTOP
OR SUMMIT   N

0   MILES   0.25

New England Trunk Line Trail, a gravel-surfaced rail-trail that stretches from Franklin to Willimantic, Ct. The route was once a line of the Hartford and New Haven Railroad and was transformed to a public trail with the help of the Rails-to-Trails Conservancy, a non-profit organization dedicated to preserving unused railroad corridors as trails. With the rails and ties removed, bridges spanning the streams, and a level and dry grade, the trail provides relatively easy biking. It runs eastward to intersect Grove St., 1.7 miles south of its intersection with Forge Hill Road.

For a 2.6-mile, intermediate-level loop follow Forge Hill Road to Spring Street, turn left and continue south for 0.8 miles, then turn left on a double-track trail known as **Hillside Place**, another of Franklin's unmaintained public roads. It runs eastward to the end of Lorraine Metcalf Rd. across a low, flat area with a rough, cobble stone finish of rocks that creates a jolting ride for bicyclists. After a half-mile Hillside Place climbs a short hill, turns hard right at an intersection, and soon ends at Lorraine Metcalf Rd. and a second trail intersection. Turn left at this second intersection and follow the trail uphill along old stone walls back to the trailhead at the top of Forge Hill.

SINGLE-TRACKS:

A great collection of motorcycle trails lies in and around this loop. Zigzagging through trees in an endless series of turns, these nameless paths are suitable for both intermediate and expert riders. The ground is surprisingly smooth but a scattering of rocks, roots, and ruts creates enjoyable obstacle courses and the slopes are gradual enough to be rideable in any direction. The cluster of trails west of Spring Street has the steepest terrain while those to the east have longer lengths on a more moderate slope.

A particularly good downhill run awaits on the path that starts near the intersection of Forge Hill Rd. and the powerline and descends eastward to Grove St. The half-mile route swerves gracefully between trees as it drops down the hill for an exciting ride.

156

DRIVING DIRECTIONS:

From Interstate 495 take Exit 17 and follow Route 140 north for one tenth of a mile. Turn left on Grove St. and continue for three tenths of a mile, then turn right on Forge Hill Rd. Park at the end beside the road, being careful not to block the gate.

PUBLIC TRANSPORTATION:

The Franklin line stops at Forge Park. From the station, turn right on Rte. 140 south and continue for a half-mile. Turn right on Grove St., then right on Forge Hill Rd. and continue to the end. Total mileage from the station to the trailhead is 1.6 miles.

BIKE SHOPS:

Bicycles Plus, 391 East Central St. (Rte. 140), Franklin, Tel. (508) 520-1212

Crossing Cycle, 282 Cottage St., Franklin, Tel. (508) 528-1010

Franklin Bicycle, 28 East Central St. (Rte. 140), Franklin, Tel. (508) 520-2453

Specialty Ski & Bike, 267 Hartford Ave. (Rte. 126), Bellingham, Tel. (508) 966-5000

ADDITIONAL INFORMATION:

Franklin State Forest, c/o F. Gilbert Hills State Forest, 45 Mill St., Foxborough, MA 02035, Tel. (508) 543-5850

Rails-to-Trails Conservancy, 1100 Seventeenth St. NW, Washington, DC 20036, Tel. (202) 331-9696

23
Wrentham State Forest
Wrentham

Wrentham State Forest's rugged single-tracks offer untold miles of mountain biking. Although some easy riding exists, the area is suited mostly to intermediate and expert riders who are ready to match their skills and energies to this vast network of demanding trails.

BACKGROUND:

This state forest was established in 1934 with a 390-acre parcel surrounding the current trailhead parking lot. It was expanded in 1936 with 543 acres to the east and eventually reached a size of 1,070 acres before construction of I-495 consumed some of the land in the 1960's. The Civilian Conservation Corps served the area during the forest's early years with road building and tree planting.

Today Wrentham State Forest remains relatively undeveloped. No facilities are present except for a parking lot, trailhead kiosk, and miles of trails open to all kinds of users including off-road motorcyclists (from May 2 to October 31) and hunters (mostly in the late fall).

TRAIL POLICIES:

This property is managed by the staff at neighboring F. Gilbert Hills State Forest in Foxborough, who ask visitors to respect the forest by leaving it as you found it for others to enjoy. Many trails are suffering from severe erosion so mountain bikers are urged not to ride during spring thaw and during or immediately after rainy periods when soils are soft and vulnerable. Since trail policies could change, read trailhead notices before you ride. The area is open from dawn to dusk.

ORIENTATION:

Finding your way through Wrentham's maze of options can be difficult because few trails have official names and even fewer have signs to display them. Newcomers should be aware that the trails' convoluted courses and tangled array of intersections make it easy to become dioriented while a lack of reliable landmarks makes one place begin to look like another. Bring a topographical map (Wrentham Quadrangle) together with the accompanying map and follow them carefully when exploring for the first time.

Two public roads divide Wrentham State Forest into three different areas for riding, and the trailhead parking lot is centrally located to give easy access to each region. The noise from one of the roadways, I-495, provides a useful means of orientation in the nearby portions of each area. The mountain biking is similar in all three with intermediate and difficult conditions prevailing.

DOUBLE-TRACKS:

Severed by construction of the highway, many of Wrentham's old forest roads no longer align in a contiguous, useable network and are now separated into dead end fragments. The rutted jeep road descending from gate 23 at the parking lot leads to such a segment. Continuing westward across several others, cross this old roadway on a short single-track that struggles over many obstacles, including a stream, turn right at the end on a double-track heading north and then take the next left on a trail that leads over a bank, skirts a meadow, and ends at an intersection of two primary double-tracks.

The **Hollow Rock Trail** runs for 1.2 miles from this point with intermediate riding conditions before it leaves the state forest at private property. It begins with a gradual, uphill grade heading west beneath a cliff, then crests the hill, descends, and levels between a line of exposed ledge and the edge of a wetland. The trail arcs northward after a half-mile and rolls and turns gently through undisturbed woodlands toward its endpoint, intersecting three single-tracks on the left that head for private property along the way. A final single-track on the right offers an intermediate-
160

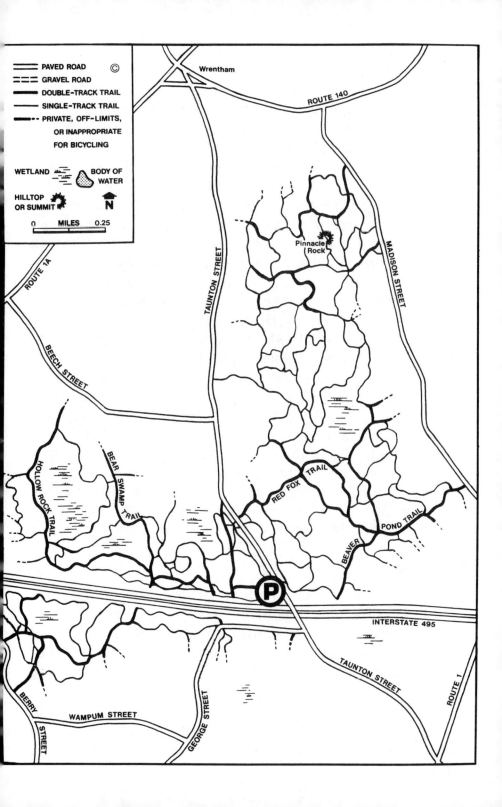

level return route.

The **Bear Swamp Trail** has a similar ride but is shorter. One of the trail"s most prominent characteristics is the large puddles that form across its width requiring cyclists to tread carefully.

Wrentham's largest area lies across Taunton St. from the parking lot, where several more miles of double-track riding await. The **Red Fox Trail** originates at gate 24 a quarter-mile from the parking lot and ventures into the woods in an area of mellow terrain, intersecting many other trails as it goes. An intermediate-level ride, it has a scattering of avoidable rocks and eventually encounters several brief, eroded slopes before dropping on a final hill to its terminus at another intersection after 0.9 miles.

Here it meets the **Beaver Pond Trail**, a similar route which begins beside I-495. Starting in relative flatness, the Beaver Pond Trail traverses an area of former farmland, now forest that is bordered by stone walls, rises over a small hill to the Red Fox Trail, circles the edge of a small bog, and then crosses a bridge over a brook where prominent ledges and an old millsite are evident. From this point the Beaver Trail turns right and then immediately left, scrambling up a loose slope between two granite outcroppings, then rolls gently for the last quarter-mile to Madison St. Much of the trail's traffic flow heads southeastward near this endpoint to a trailhead off Madison St. that is outside the state forest boundary.

SINGLE-TRACKS:

It is the winding motorcycle trails that draw most mountain bikers to Wrentham. Nameless and unmarked, these paths traverse a vast area of oak forest, small wetlands, and rocky hills that rise from the forest floor like huge domes of granite. Many have intermediate-level riding as they weave between trees and exposed rocks with a confined width that is knee-deep in blueberry bushes. Others deserve a difficult rating as they scramble up and drop off a grueling supply of hills and ledges that have long

162

been suffering from motorcycle-induced erosion, while a few others are simply unrideable for most mortals. Since Wrentham's motorcycle paths have no means of identification, readers must discover for themselves their routes of choice.

The steep path winding along the ridgeline of **Pinnacle Rock** at the forest's northern reach is an exciting trip, although it is nearly impossible to ride its entire length. The treeless ledges passed along the way allow nice views at several points.

The single-tracks that are south of I-495 are difficult routes but worth a try for experts. Accessed by George St., they overlap a few double-tracks with a grueling supply of steep slopes, exposed rocks, and plenty of turns. The smaller size of this neighborhood of trails makes it easier to navigate but noise from the highway unfortunately is never far away.

DRIVING DIRECTIONS:
From I-495 take Exit 14B for Rte. 1 south. Continue for a half-mile to the first traffic signal and turn right on Taunton St. Look for the trailhead parking lot 0.9 miles ahead on the left.

BIKE SHOPS:
Bicycles Plus, 391 E. Central St. (Rte. 140), Franklin, Tel. (508) 520-1212

Crossing Cycle, 282 Cottage St., Franklin, Tel. (508) 528-1010

Epicycle, 345 E. Washington St. (Rte. 1), North Attleboro, Tel. (508) 643-2453

Franklin Bicycle, 28 E. Central St. (Rte. 140), Franklin, Tel. (508) 520-2453

Mountain Bikes & More, 10 Commercial St. (Rte. 140), Foxborough, Tel. (508) 543-3833

Sirois Bicycle, 893 Landry Ave., North Attleboro, Tel. (508) 695-6303

ADDITIONAL INFORMATION:
Wrentham State Forest, c/o F. Gilbert Hills State Forest, 45 Mill St., Foxborough, MA 02035, Tel. (508) 543-5850

24
F. Gilbert Hills State Forest
Foxborough

An especially popular spot for mountain biking, F. Gilbert Hills State Forest and Foxborough conservation lands preserve a large area of trails near the intersection of interstates 95 and 495. Riders have the choice between cruising 10 miles of easy and intermediate woods roads or clawing their way through 10 miles of difficult single-track.

BACKGROUND:

Named after a dedicated state forester, F. Gilbert Hills State Forest originated with a 300-acre purchase in 1926, grew substantially during the 1930's, and gained 172 acres in 1986 to create a preserve of over 1,000 acres. The forest served as a camp for the Civilian Conservation Corps during the Great Depression when workers constructed the roads, planted trees, and dug water holes for fire fighting purposes.

TRAIL POLICIES:

The forest's trail policy permits mountain biking on all double-track routes unless they are specifically posted as being closed to bicycles, and on single-tracks that are specifically posted as being open to bicycles. These single-tracks are clearly marked by green, triangular tree tags bearing the image of a bicycle for one-way traffic in the counter-clockwise direction. Mountain biking is prohibited on single-tracks that do not have these green markers.

F. Gilbert Hills attracts a wide variety of activities including hiking, horseback riding, and (between May 1 and November 1) off-road motorcycling, and to accommodate them all the state forest staff has designated single-track loops for each user group. Other trails are multi-use and the forest supervisor warns mountain bikers to show courtesy when riding them. Travel at a safe speed and avoid startling people by announcing your presence well in advance.

Signs posted at intersections identify the majority of woods roads, and green tree tags mark the single-tracks that are open for biking. In addition, a numbered sign is posted at each water hole and displayed on the accompanying map, so bring it along if you are exploring for the first time.

Wolf Meadow Road, 1.1-miles long, is the main route from the forest headquarters trailhead. It encounters a few uphill slopes that require extra energy and careful pedaling over loose stones, but is a mostly easy ride through a variety of natural scenes.

It ends at **High Rock Road**, the 2.2-mile backbone of the forest's trail system. Mild terrain and a smooth surface make the distance east to Lakeview Road an easy ride while bigger hills and a loose, eroded surface prevail to the west. Lyons Falls, a small waterfall near waterhole 4, sits at an open slab of ledge on one of these slopes but the brook is typically dry for much of the year. High Rock Road continues past the falls on its toughest uphill battle, a quarter-mile scramble over loose rocks and sand, then levels before reaching 430' High Rock, one of the forest's highest points. Unfortunately trees block the views. The road's final mile is a paved descent to Rte. 1 that is occasionally used by cars.

Two intermediate-level loops can be made from the parking lot using these and other forest roads. One combines Wolf Meadow Road, High Rock Road, and the **Megley Trail** for a 4.2-mile ride. The mile-long Megley Trail intersects High Rock Road on the long hill above Lyons Falls, rolls with a few eroded hills in an oak forest, and then descends to the shade of pines. Turn left at the end on West St. and left on Mill St. to return to the parking lot.

A second loop combines Wolf Rock Road, High Rock Road, and **Messenger Road** for a 4.3-mile ride. Messenger Road departs High Rock Road a short distance above the

166

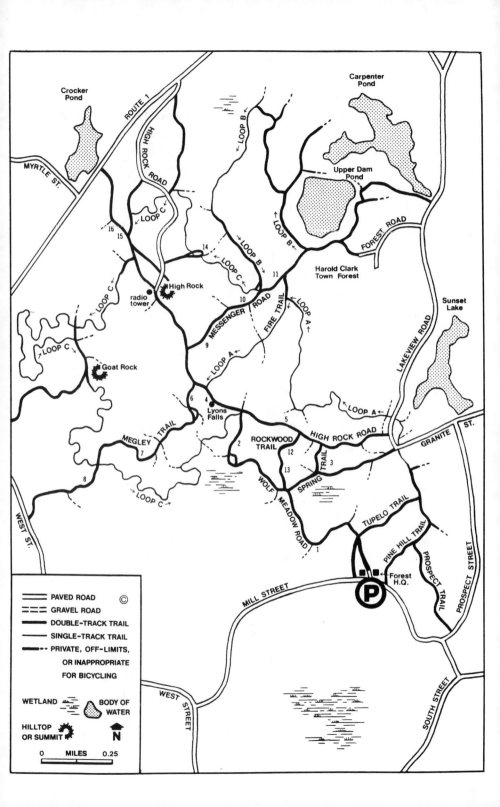

Megley Trail and runs northward with an alternating pattern of rough slopes and smooth flats to Upper Dam Pond in the Harold Clark Town Forest. Turning eastward, it soon emerges on pavement at the end of Forest Rd. To finish the loop, ride Forest Rd. to its origin at Lakeview Rd., turn right and continue southward to a ninety-degree left turn where Granite St. begins. Turn right at this point on an unnamed woods road, then left on **Spring Trail** and left on Wolf Meadow Road to return to the trailhead.

SINGLE-TRACKS:

The highlight to mountain biking at Gilbert Hills for many riders is the thrill of the single-tracks. Divided into three loops, these difficult paths were originally created by off-road motorcycles and follow convoluted courses of sharp hills and dizzying switchbacks in a landscape where huge, glacial boulders loom beside the trail and an abundance of smaller rocks disrupt the treadway. While some sections explore remote corners of the property, others intersect and overlap woods roads that provide useful short-cuts.

Loop A is 3.6 miles long. It begins at the trailhead on Wolf Rock Road, turns right on the double-track **Tupelo Trail**, then left at the end on a path that crosses the pavement of Granite St. and Lakeview Rd. The trail becomes difficult at this point, topping two small hills where erosion has left big rocks and roots in the way, then continues over more gradual slopes and a few flat sections to the **Fire Trail** at the half-way mark. Turning left, Loop A returns to the south with a final half-mile segment of single-track that ends with a rocky descent to High Rock Road just above Lyons Falls, 1.3 miles from the trailhead.

The 3.7-mile **Loop B** begins where Loop A turns left on the Fire Trail. Turning to the right, Loop B soon reaches Messenger Road, turns right, then left just before Upper Dam Pond on a trail that climbs a gradual slope with exposed rocks. After several more left-hand turns the loop circles back to the south after 0.9 miles, returning to Messenger Road through flatter terrain with numerous mud holes. The final 2 miles back to the trailhead follow Messenger, High Rock, and Wolf Meadow roads.

Loop C measures 6.5 miles and begins where Loop B first meets Messenger Road. Turning left where Loop B turns right, Loop C follows Messenger Road south for a short distance and then diverges on a single-track that climbs a small hill and descends to the circular turn-around of a dead end woods road. Crossing it, the path tops two more hills, continues across the pavement of High Rock Road, and circles the northern slope of High Rock. After following a utility line along a service road toward the summit, Loop C turns right and resumes its rocky, winding character for the next 3 miles, passing beneath Goat Rock and crossing the Megley Trail along the way. Where it emerges at the intersection of High Rock and Wolf Meadow roads, turn right to return to the trailhead, 1.1 miles away.

DRIVING DIRECTIONS:

From I-95 take Exit 7B and follow Rte. 140 north for a short distance, then take the first left on Walnut St. Continuing straight through a four-way intersection, follow Walnut St. to the end, then turn left on South St. After a quarter-mile turn right on Mill St. and find the trailhead parking lots a half-mile ahead on both sides of the road.

BIKE SHOPS:

Bicycles Plus, 391 E. Central St. (Rte. 140), Franklin, Tel. (508) 520-1212

Crossing Cycle, 282 Cottage St., Franklin, Tel. (508) 528-1010

Epicycle, 345 E. Washington St. (Rte. 1), North Attleboro, Tel. (508) 643-2453

Franklin Bicycle, 22 E. Central St. (Rte. 140), Franklin, Tel. (508) 520-2453

Mountain Bikes & More, 10 Commercial St. (Rte. 140), Foxborough, Tel. (508) 543-3833

Sirois Bicycle, 893 Landry Ave., North Attleboro, Tel. (508) 695-6303

ADDITIONAL INFORMATION:

F. Gilbert Hills State Forest, 45 Mill St., Foxborough, MA 02035, Tel. (508) 543-5850

25
Noanet Woodlands Reservation
Dover

Native Americans referred to this area as *Peculiar Hunting Place* and today mountain bikers feel some of the same sentiments. Noanet's strict rules and regulated approach to the use of mountain bikes is unique in the Boston area but the reservation's beautiful natural features are a worthy reward. Most routes are double-track with either easy or intermediate conditions.

BACKGROUND:

Noanet Woodlands is a property of the Trustees of Reservations, a private conservation foundation that has been preserving the Massachusetts landscape for over 100 years. This reservation was established in 1984 after a bequest from Amelia Peabody and, together with neighboring parcels donated by Olivia and Henry Cabot, totals 591 acres. The Trustees of Reservations is a non-profit organization and welcomes donations, which can be left in a contribution box near the trailhead.

TRAIL POLICIES:

Mountain biking is highly regulated at Noanet and it is important that cyclists understand and respect the rules. Located only a short distance from Rte. 128, these trails have long been a popular place to hike, jog, and horseback ride and the appearance of mountain bikes has strained capacity. The managers of the property suggest mountain biking only as an alternative means of using the trails.

The regulations require that bicyclists first purchase a permit at the trailhead ranger station, which is open only on weekends and holidays. Good for the calendar year, the permit must be shown on weekends but is not required for riding on weekdays. Additionally, mountain biking is prohibited before 11:00AM on Saturdays and Sundays.

Unless otherwise posted, mountain bikes are prohibited on the trails between March 1 and April 30 each spring and during the winter when conditions permit cross country skiing. Bicyclists should remain on the trails and obey trail closures. Competitive and reckless riding, high speeds, and groups of five or more are prohibited. The Trustee's list of general regulations prohibits *conduct that disturbs the tranquility of the reservation or its enjoyment by others*. Please ride responsibly.

Since these policies could change, be sure to check trailhead notices before you ride.

ORIENTATION:

Noanet Woodlands is a particularly well-kept place complete with a trailhead ranger station and information kiosk. Three color-coded routes explore the property with consecutively numbered intersections that are displayed on the map to help visitors determine their location. Signs bearing the *no bikes* symbol mark trails that are closed to bicycling and the reservation's boundaries are clearly posted on peripheral routes.

Trailhead parking is in **Caryl Park**, a property owned by the town of Dover at the northern end of the trail system. Two easy trails leave the parking lot and deliver visitors to the Noanet Woodlands boundary at intersection 3 after a half-mile.

DOUBLE-TRACKS:

Here the reservation's three marked trails diverge on separate courses to their common endpoint at intersection 18. The 1.2-mile **Peabody Trail**, marked in blue, is the easiest option as it remains in the relative flatness of the valley floor at the center of the property. Named for the woman who donated most of this land, the trail begins with a short, uphill slope rippled with tree roots, then flattens at the top with a smoother surface. After passing through a meadow it descends to a pond where a dam and millsite mark the former location of the Dover Union Iron Company

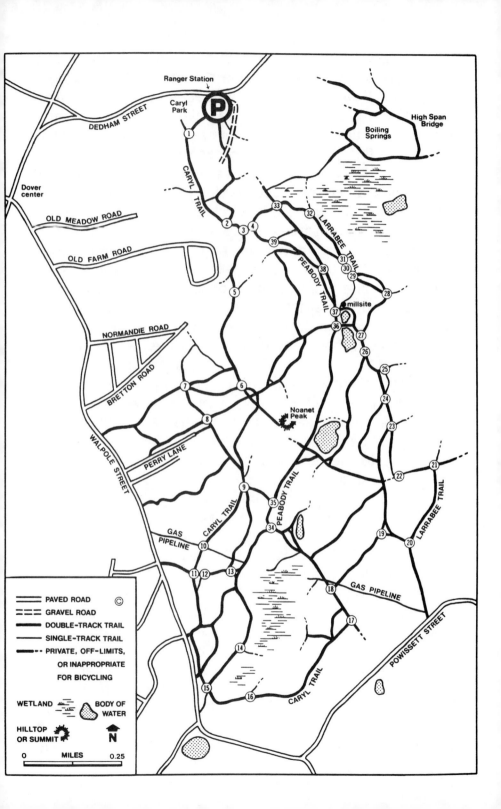

which operated a water wheel in the mid-1800's to process iron. The stone remains of the mill are worth stopping to see. The Peabody Trail continues with a gently rolling course and a smooth, gravelly finish past several other ponds, then turns eastward at intersection 34 and the 1-mile mark. The final stretch to intersection 18 has several hills.

The **Caryl Trail**, the reservation's longest marked route, takes a disjointed course along the western boundary. Tree roots grasp the entire width of this double-track and rocks bulge from its surface in places so expect an intermediate ride from maneuvering around a steady stream of bumps. The trail's round, yellow markers begin in Caryl Park. The first half-mile is an obstacle-free cruise but the trail gets rougher at intersection 3, rising for the next half-mile to intersection 6. It turns right and descends briefly to intersection 7, then bears left and resumes a steady, uphill tack for the next third of a mile, passing several spurs connecting Walpole St. before cresting the slope near intersection 9. Here the trail flattens, crosses the treeless corridor of a gas pipeline, and turns left at intersection 11. After a brief descent to 13, the Caryl Trail follows the edge of a wetland to the reservation's southern border, 2.5 miles from the parking lot.

Turning eastward, it then traces the boundary beside the fields of horse farms off Powissett St. until intersection 17, where it turns left on an old farm road and ends at intersection 18 after a total of 3.2 miles.

Bicyclists can return on the 1.7-mile **Larrabee Trail** to complete a 4.9-mile loop. The Larrabee Trail, marked in red, includes a combination of double- and single-track and involves all levels of riding ability, from easy to difficult. A few sections are narrow and rough but these are confined to short distances and can easily be walked. From intersection 18 the trail rolls smoothly over grassy double-tracks for a half-mile to intersection 21 where it turns and climbs a small but challenging hill to an open ledge. A trail posted as off-limits to bicycling intersects on the left at this point. The

Larrabee Trail descends northward to intersection 25, turns left, and approaches the ponds above the millsite. After an eroded downhill run to 28, it follows gentler terrain for the final half-mile back to intersection 4. Tree roots from surrounding pines make much of this last leg a bumpy ride.

One of the reservation's highlights is riding to the top of 387' **Noanet Peak** where an open ledge offers an inspiring, 180-degree view. The skyline of Boston, 19 miles away, cuts the horizon to the northeast. Note that bicyclists are permitted to use only one of the trails on Noanet Peak and that the others are posted off-limits. The trail that is open for bicycling climbs directly from the Caryl Trail at intersection 6 with an eroded surface near the top which can easily be walked.

DRIVING DIRECTIONS:

From Rte. 128 take Exit 16B and follow Rte. 109 west for 0.7 miles to Summer St. Turn right and drive for 1.2 miles to the end, then turn left on Westfield St. and drive for 0.7 miles to the end. Turn left on Dedham St. and look for the parking lot at Caryl Park 1.9 miles ahead on the left.

BIKE SHOPS:

Dedham Bike, 403 Washington St., Dedham, Tel. (781) 326-1531

Fat Dog Pro Shop, 940 High St., Westwood, Tel. (781) 251-9447

Norwood Bicycle Depot, 85 Broadway, Norwood, Tel. (781) 762-2112

St. Moritz Sports, 475 Washington St., Wellesley, Tel. (781) 235-6669

Town & Country Bicycles, 67 North St., Medfield, Tel. (508) 359-8377

ADDITIONAL INFORMATION:

The Trustees of Reservations, 572 Essex St., Beverly, MA 01915, Tel. (978) 921-1944

26
Borderland State Park
Easton

The mountain biking at Borderland has a split personality. Four miles of easy carriage roads circle the flat area of the park's ponds and fields while a network of tough single-tracks twist through the rocks and trees of the surrounding hills. Measure your mood and ride accordingly.

BACKGROUND:

Before the state acquired this property in 1971 it had been the private estate of Oakes and Blanch Ames, both members of prominent Massachusetts families. The three-story, stone mansion standing at the park's main entrance is a testiment to their prosperity and lends a dignified atmosphere to the start of any trail excursion. Tours of the building are periodically scheduled. The Ames named their 1,250-acre estate *Borderland* for its position on the town line between Easton and Sharon, and today the park bearing this name is an asset for many activities. With recent gifts and acquisitions it now measures 1,772 acres in size.

TRAIL POLICIES:

Borderland State Park permits mountain biking on all routes except the **Pond Edge Trail**, **Swamp Trail**, and **Quiet Woods Trail**. When approaching other trail users, mountain bikers must slow to a minimum safe operating speed, yield the trail, and not pass unless it is safe to do so. The park gets large numbers of walkers, especially on weekends, so expect to encounter people and be courteous when you do. Since additional trail closures and policy changes could occur, stop at the trailhead notice board before you ride.

All visitors to Borderland should know that the park is open only during the daytime and that the gates to parking lots are locked each night. Closing time varies with the seasons but is posted at points of access, so be alert for the schedule and plan your ride carefully. A large bell on the roof of the mansion sounds fifteen minutes before closing. Pets are welcome but must be leashed.

ORIENTATION:

Two parking lots serve Borderland. The most popular one is off Massapoag Ave. on the western side of the park where a broad lawn spreads between the Ames Mansion and the visitor center attracting picnickers and sunbathers. The park's two main carriage roads depart from this point and access all the outlying trails.

Trails are named and well marked with signs at intersections and maps are stationed at some locations to help visitors find their way. The carriage roads around the ponds have easy biking while the outlying single-tracks have intermediate and difficult conditions.

DOUBLE-TRACKS:

The 2.7-mile **Leach Pond Loop** is one of the park's prettiest and most popular options. It circles Leach Pond with a smooth surface, beautiful views of ponds and fields, and gentle hills that are brief so the riding is suitable for all abilities. The loop begins at the lawn near the visitor center and descends to the shoreline where it rolls and turns through the woods for a half-mile. Turning right at the first major intersection, it crosses a wooden bridge over a spillway below Upper Leach Pond and continues along Long Dam to the next intersection in a field at the 1.2-mile mark. Turning right again, the loop reaches the secondary trailhead parking lot at the farm house in another half-mile, then turns right for the final mile-long leg back to the mansion.

Extend this ride for an additional half-mile by continuing around Upper Leach Pond to Mountain St. At the Tisdale Homesite, a meadow that was once a small farm, turn right on the paved road and look for a metal gate and woods road a short distance ahead on the right. This easy

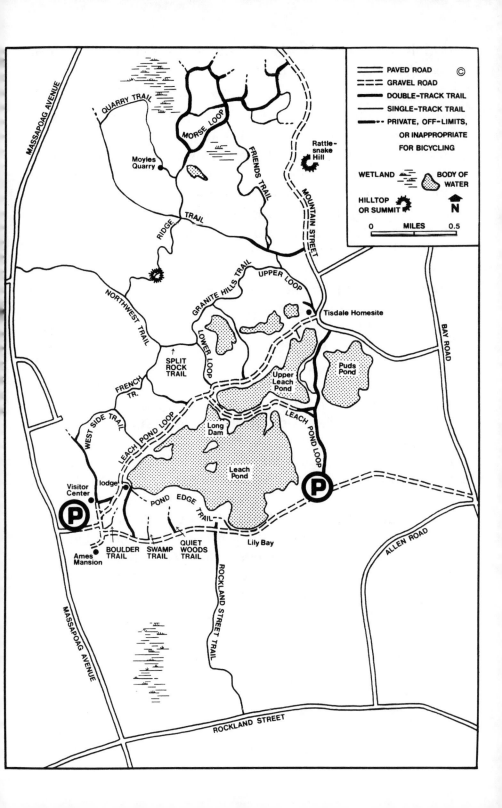

double-track trail passes the edge of Puds Pond before joining the Leach Pond Loop.

Look to Borderland's single-tracks to provide more excitement. The 0.8-mile **West Side Trail**, one of the mildest options, begins at the visitor center and rises on a gentle grade for the first quarter-mile, then bends right and narrows with more difficult conditions. After a half-mile it intersects the **French Trail**, an ambitious route that climbs to an open ledge and encounters an unrideable section of rocks. It ends on the **Northwest Trail**, a well-worn, rocky course that struggles up a boulder-strewn hill on its way from the Leach Pond Loop to Massapoag Ave., 1 mile north of Borderland's main entrance.

The brief **Split Rock Trail** links the Northwest with the aptly named **Granite Hills Trail** which explores more rugged terrain with a gnarly course of boulders and ledge. It is divided into two portions, mile-long Lower Loop and the steeper and more treacherous 0.7-mile Upper Loop.

The 1.5-mile **Ridge Trail** completes a longer ride and links several more routes in the park's most remote area. Requiring high levels of strength and skill, the trail sneaks between trees and boulders with barely the space for a bicycle as it winds through an area of scrub oak forest and open ledge at some of Borderland's highest elevations. Starting at the Northwest Trail, the first half tackles the roughest surfaces and steepest terrain while the second half enjoys a gradual descent on an old wagon road.

Pedaling the **Quarry Trail** is a more relaxing affair. It follows the faint remains of several wagon roads and allows smooth passage for bikes in most places with the exception of a few mudholes and rocky spots. Along the way watch for Moyles Quarry, a source of granite in the early 1800's. The remote **Morse Loop** is one of the park's easiest to ride with gentle terrain and a firm surface.

Alone at the southern end of the park, the 1.5-mile **Rockland Street Trail** intersects the Leach Pond Loop near

Lily Bay and runs southward to Rockland St., 1.5 miles away from the mansion by pavement. Lots of tree roots and a few wet spots make it a challenging ride.

DRIVING DIRECTIONS:

From I-95, take Exit 9 (if northbound) or Exit 10 (if southbound) and follow signs to Rte. 27. Drive south on Rte. 27 to the traffic signal at Sharon center, continue straight through the intersection, then turn immediately right on Pond St. Drive for 0.9 miles to a rotary beside Massapoag Lake and continue straight through on Massapoag Ave. for 3.5 miles to the park entrance, on the left.

From I-495, take Exit 10 and follow Rte. 123 east for 3.6 miles. Turn left on Poquanticut Ave. and continue for 1.3 miles, then turn left on Massapoag Ave. The park entrance is 2.1 miles ahead on the right.

PUBLIC TRANSPORTATION:

The Attleboro/Stoughton line stops at Sharon. From the station find Rte. 27 (Depot St.) which crosses a bridge over the tracks. Turn right and ride uphill to the center traffic signal, continue straight through the intersection, then turn immediately right on Pond St. Ride for 0.9 miles to a rotary and continue straight on Massapoag Ave. for 3.5 miles to the park entrance on the left. The total distance is 4.8 miles.

BIKE SHOPS:

Landry's Bicycles, 574 Washington St. (Rte. 138), Easton, Tel. (508) 230-8882

Mountain Bikes & More, 10 Commercial St. (Rte. 140), Foxborough, Tel. (508) 543-3833

Travis Cycle, 722 N. Main St., Brockton, Tel. (508) 586-6394

ADDITIONAL INFORMATION:

Borderland State Park, Massapoag Ave., North Easton, MA 02356, Tel. (508) 238-6566

27
Blue Hills Reservation
Milton

One of eastern Massachusetts' biggest parks sprawls beside the city of Boston with miles of trails, acres of solitude, and hilltop vistas. Mostly double-track, the riding at Blue Hills is hilly and ranges from easy to difficult.

BACKGROUND:

The Blue Hills Reservation was created in 1893 as one of the first acquisitions of the Metropolitan Parks System, now the Metropolitan District Commission (MDC), under the leadership of renowned landscape architect Charles Eliot. Measuring over 7,000 acres, the reservation offers a swimming lake, picnicking area, museum, golf course, summer camps, downhill ski area, and a 125-mile trail system through a chain of 22 hills.

TRAIL POLICIES:

Mountain biking is permitted only on certain trails in certain parts of the Blue Hills Reservation. Because it is a heavily visited, multi-use area, the MDC has established a specific policy that allows mountain biking in the region north of I-93 and west of Rte. 28. Most of these trails appear on the accompanying map but additional mountain biking trails lie to the west near Little Blue Hill and Foul Meadow. Signs bearing the *no bikes* symbol designate certain trails within this area as being off-limits for reasons of soil erosion, public safety, or habitat protection.

In addition, mountain biking is prohibited between January 1 and April 15 each year when trail surfaces are vulnerable to ruts and erosion. During the remainder of the year, cyclists are urged not to ride when the trails are wet.

The MDC staff reminds riders that their cooperation with these policies will help preserve the future of mountain biking at Blue Hills. Much of the credit for this multi-use approach belongs to the New England Mountain Bike Association (NEMBA) which has assisted with trail maintenance, helped to create a mountain biking brochure for the reservation, and coordinates the volunteer *Trailwatch* patrol to monitor the trails and educate riders. NEMBA urges bicyclists to wear helmets, ride at safe speeds, and to yield to hikers and horseback riders. Since future policy changes are possible, watch for trailhead notices or stop by Reservation Headquarters at 695 Hillside St.

ORIENTATION:

The vast size and countless intersections of the Blue Hills trail system deserve respect. Visitors are fortunate to find trail maps stationed at various points throughout the reservation, granite posts inscribed with trail names at roadway crossings, and numbered intersections that are displayed on the map. Plot your progress carefully when exploring for the first time.

The topography is dominated by a spine of hills that form an east-west ridgeline along the center of the reservation. In general, the trails that parallel this ridgeline encounter milder slopes while the trails that run perpendicular to it, in the north-south direction, encounter bigger ones as they ascend and descend the elevation.

DOUBLE-TRACKS:

A popular, centrally located place to start a ride is Houghtons Pond where a visitor center, swimming beach, and restrooms are located. An easy trail circles the water but note that bicycles are not permitted on the portion that parallels the beach on the northern shore.

The nearby **Bugbee Path** is a primary trail through this area and stretches for 1.6 miles from Reservation Headquarters eastward to Rte. 28 offering an easy ride with the exception of a few rocky slopes. To find it from the Houghtons Pond parking lot, follow **Headquarters Path** northward along Hillside St. for a quarter-mile and Bugbee Path starts on the right, just before a horse paddock. It begins with a gravel surface, then joins a paved road that is closed to traffic and follows it uphill to a cleared area where the pavement crests and descends to the right. Here the Bugbee Path continues straight, rolling and turning in the shade of woods for another 1.3 miles.

Trails intersecting Bugbee Path on the right descend southward to **Old Blue Hill River Road**, a stretch of pavement severed by construction of I-93. The intermediate **Angle Path** has a moderate slope with exposed rocks while the **Burnt Hill Path** drops over steeper pitches with a rougher surface. The grassy **Beech Hollow Path** allows the easiest ride but it too has a few rocky spots.

Trails intersecting Bugbee Path on the left ascend the ridgeline to the north. An exception to this is the **Tucker Hill Path** which offers a flat and firm surface for all but a brief distance at its northern endpoint. Both the **Dark Hollow Path** and the **Doe Hollow Path** climb through passes between hilltops and then descend to Chickatawbut Rd., encountering rocky surfaces along the way. Lined by a stone wall, the **Forest Path** is a smoother way over the ridge from the end of the Bugbee to the Headquarters Path.

An intermediate-level, 4-mile loop circles this area from the parking lot. Follow the Headquarters Path to Bugbee Path and ride to Rte. 28, turn left and take the Forest Path to intersection 2175, then turn left on the Headquarters Path which returns to the parking lot. Where the Headquarters Path crosses Chickatawbut Rd. and becomes a difficult single-track, turn left and follow the pavement for a short distance. Watch for the path crossing back to the left after a right-hand turn in the road.

A scenic diversion from this loop is the half-mile ride up **Buck Hill** where an unbroken view awaits. Not to be confused with the Buck Hill Trail, this unnamed route begins on Headquarters Path at intersection 2160 and takes a direct route up the fall-line, scrambling through a dry streambed of loose rocks. The slope is manageable but it is a challenging trip heading both up and down.

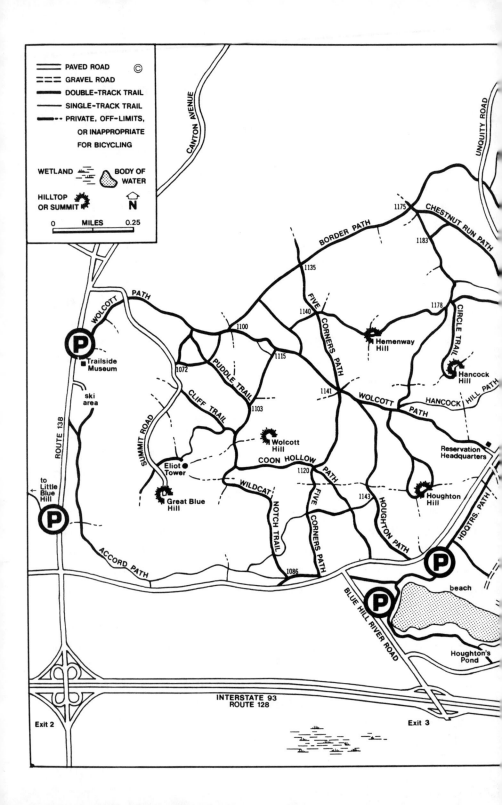

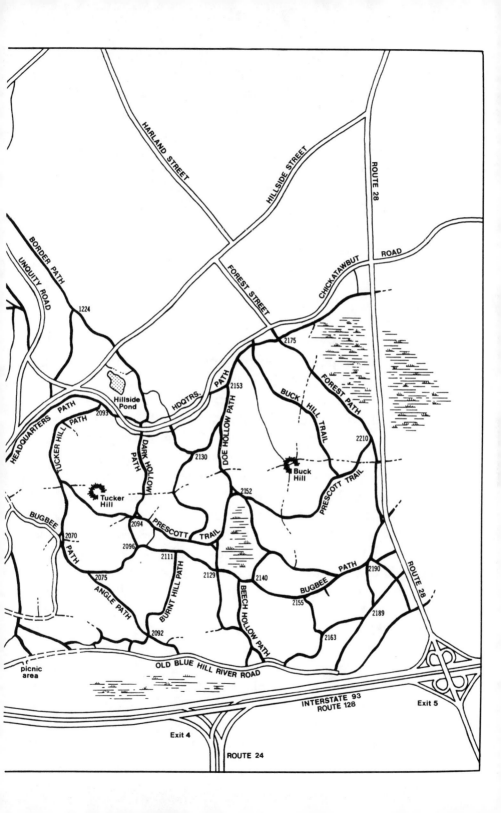

West of Hillside St. is an area where mountain biking trails conquer even bigger hills. The smoothest, widest option is the 1.5-mile **Wolcott Path**, a primary route that climbs for a half-mile from Reservation Headquarters, descends slightly to a major intersection (#1141) known as Five Corners, then continues over flat ground until it drops on a rocky course to Rte. 138 near the Trailside Museum.

Wolcott Path serves as the first leg of an easy, 3-mile loop. Ride it from Headquarters for 1 mile to intersection 1100 and turn right on **Border Path**, a similar trail following the reservation's northern boundary. At intersection 1175, where Border Path descends to Unquity Rd., turn right on **Chestnut Run Path**, a level course along a sidehill that ends on Unquity Rd., then turn right and follow the pavement back to Headquarters.

The reservation's biggest climb is 635' **Great Blue Hill**, the highest point on the Atlantic Coast south of Maine. The paved **Summit Road** rises from Rte. 138 to the top in less than a mile and provides beautiful views of the Boston skyline, Atlantic Ocean, and mounts Monadnock and Wachusett on the clearest days. Be cautious when riding down Summit Road since it is frequently used by walkers.

Expert riders can try descending the summit on the **Coon Hollow Path**, a rough trail with steep slopes. It begins in front of the Eliot Tower and drops quickly over ledges for the first quarter-mile, then reaches milder terrain in a notch between Great Blue Hill and Wolcott Hill. Descending more moderately, the trail alternates between level, smooth stretches and steep, rocky pitches before it ends on Hillside St. Beware of the water bars dug across the trail. Parallel **Wildcat Notch Path** and **Houghton Path** drop down the same slope with similar conditions.

Farther to the west, the area of **Little Blue Hill** offers an intermediate-level, 2.2-mile loop for mountain biking from the Park & Ride lot on Rte. 138. A confusing tangle of footpaths laces through the trees beyond the trailhead sign and cyclists should keep to the right bearing north along the base of the hill. Bicycles are not permitted at the top of Little Blue Hill but they can reach the end of the Moulton Path where a stone bench and distant view await.

The Fowl Meadow area presents the Blue Hill's flattest, easiest place to ride. Alone at the reservation's western reach, the Burma Road travels a 2-mile, straight-line course through pretty scenery of semi-open wetlands along the Neponset River that ends beside the interstate.

SINGLE-TRACKS;

Single-track riding at Blue Hills is scarce and generally requires expert riding skills. The 1.3-mile **Accord Path** starts at the ski area with a wide surface but narrows to a steep, treacherous course over jagged rocks at the base of Great Blue Hill. The **Hancock Hill Path** provides a similar experience with an eastward view from Hancock Hill.

DRIVING DIRECTIONS:

The reservation is accessed from I-93/Rte. 128 by exits 2, 3, and 5. To reach Houghton's Pond, take Exit 3 and follow Blue Hill River Rd. north for a half-mile, then turn right and continue for 3 tenths of a mile. To park near the Trailside Museum, take Exit 2 and follow Rte. 138 north for 1.2 miles. Look for the parking lot on the right after the museum.

BIKE SHOPS:

Bike Express, 96 N. Main St. (Rte. 28), Randolph, Tel. (781) 961-2453

Dave's Bike Infirmary, 440 Granite Ave., Milton, Tel. (617) 696-6123

Dedham Bike, 403 Washington St., Dedham, Tel. (781) 326-1531

Norwood Bicycle Depot, 85 Broadway, Norwood, Tel. (781) 762-2112

Quincy Cycle, 247 Quincy Ave., Quincy, Tel. (617) 471-2321

Ski Market, 400 Franklin St., Braintree, Tel. (781) 848-3733

ADDITIONAL INFORMATION:

Blue Hills Reservation, 695 Hillside St., Milton, MA 02186, Tel. (617) 698-1802

NEMBA, (800) 57-NEMBA or web: www.nemba.org

28
Ames Nowell State Park
Abington

The relaxing atmosphere at Ames Nowell's trailhead belies the struggle to be found along its trails. As picnickers sit in the shade above a lakeside view, mountain bikers battle 15 miles of rutted jeep roads and testy single-tracks that offer mostly intermediate and advanced riding.

BACKGROUND:

This state park was originally known as the Perigrine White Bird Sanctuary, a wildlife preserve established by Dr. Ames Nowell of nearby Brockton. It now measures 600 acres and attracts not only bird lovers but also large numbers of other visitors during the summer season when families come to picnic and fishermen cast for bass and pickerel. Although the park's periphery has suffered from illicit dumping of refuse, the trailhead area has been attractively developed to include picnic areas and a pavilion, toilet facilities during the warm season, and a boat launch.

TRAIL POLICIES:

All trails are open to mountain biking at the time of publication. Cyclists should be reminded that the routes in the vicinity of the trailhead can be busy so ride cautiously and be ready to yield the trail to walkers. The more distant areas of the park receive much less use but the staff urges mountain bikers riding anywhere to travel at safe speeds and to use common sense.

The park is officially open from 8:00 AM to 8:00 PM daily and the parking lot is locked each night. Swimming is not permitted in the pond.

ORIENTATION:

The trails at Ames Nowell are unnamed and unmarked so bring a map along when exploring for the first time. Several prominent natural and man-made features provide landmarks along the way and include two sets of utility corridors, roadways that border the park's west and north sides, and the open water of Cleveland Pond. A small amount of easy riding exists on some gravel roads but the majority of mountain biking routes are either intermediate double-tracks or difficult single-tracks.

GRAVEL ROADS:

If you are looking for a short warm-up or a nearly effortless cruise, begin on the gravel road that extends along the eastern shoreline of Cleveland Pond. Starting from the picnic area near the parking lot, this road offers an obstacle-free, 0.7-mile ride in the shade of woods to an isolated cove at the northern end of the pond. Hills are mild and the surface alternates between fine gravel and crushed stone. Since this route leads directly from the picnic area it is often traveled by hikers and dog-walkers on the park's busiest days.

DOUBLE-TRACKS:

Cross the bridge along the **dam** to find double-tracks spreading westward. Recently rebuilt, the dam that contains Cleveland Pond was originally constructed in the 1830's to power a small mill and flooded nearly 100 acres of farmland with an average of four feet of water. This shallow depth allows boaters to occasionally see stone walls beneath the surface.

After crossing the dam bear right on a double-track that climbs a small hill with a few water bars. This 0.9-mile trail quickly descends a rocky slope back to the shoreline and then mellows, taking a flat course through an oak forest as it winds between obstacles including puddles and avoidable rocks. At the trail's midpoint a **boardwalk** crosses a boggy cove to provide a welcome view of the surroundings and the trail eventually dead-ends beside lily pads at the shoreline of the pond .

The alternate route leading from the dam is a direct way to reach the park's outer network. Some sections of

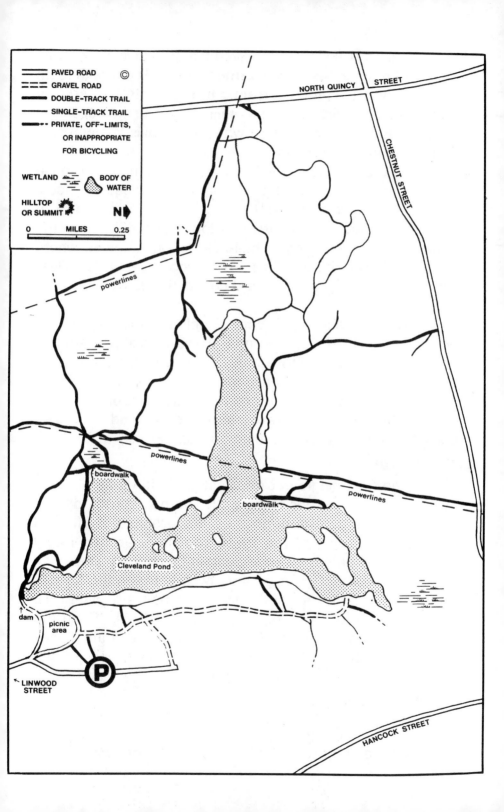

this trail are a difficult ride because the ground is strewn with rocks but other areas offer intermediate conditions with room to maneuver in gentle terrain. It intersects two sets of **powerlines**, the first at the half-mile point and the second at the park boundary to the west where the trail is less-traveled and somewhat overgrown.

Rutted jeep roads follow the open corridors of these powerlines with demanding hill climbs and loose surfaces. The trail along the first set is severed by a long arm of Cleveland Pond and requires a detour, but continues on the opposite shore for another half-mile to Chestnut St. where deep sand mires bicycle tires. The second set has a milder slope and provides a northward connection to North Quincy St.

The map shows a second double-track linking the two powerlines. Unnamed, this trail allows a relatively smooth ride in the shade of more oak forest, a welcome relief in summer from the barren environment of the utility corridors. Its slopes are mild and there is plenty of room to steer around the rocks but a few major puddles and mudholes could be hindrances, depending on water levels.

SINGLE-TRACKS:

The best single-tracks are clustered in a 2-mile loop in the northwest corner of the park and hold mostly difficult mountain biking. Although they are prohibited, off-road motorcycles frequent the trails and have eroded many areas. These paths are knee-deep in blueberry bushes and leave little room for error as they twist between the forest's trees and scale the rocky terrain in the park's highest hills, requiring high levels of both strength and skill. Even the most ambitious mountain bikers will find many of the slopes too steep to pedal. Note that the path connecting a dead end double-track at the western reach of Cleveland Pond crosses an extended wet area.

Closer to the trailhead, the single-track along the eastern shore of the pond is a difficult ride. This path is laced with tree roots and is often busy with foot traffic.

From Rte. 128 take Exit 5A for Rte. 28 south and drive for 3 miles to the center of Randolph. Turn left (east) on Rte. 139 and continue for 4 miles and, just after the Abington town line, turn right on Hancock St. After 1.9 miles turn right on Rockland St., drive 0.4 miles to the end, and turn right on Linwood St. The park's entrance is a half-mile ahead at the end of the road.

BIKE SHOPS:

Bike Barn, 242 Bedford St. (Rte. 18), Whitman, Tel. (781) 447-4469

Bike Express, 96 N. Main St. (Rte. 28), Randolph, Tel. (781) 961-2453

Les Bowles & Cyclery, 800 Brockton Ave. (Rte. 123), Abington, Tel. (781) 857-2453

Travis Cycle, 722 N. Main St., Brockton, Tel. (508) 586-6394

ADDITIONAL INFORMATION:

Ames Nowell State Park, RFD Linwood St., Abington, MA 02351, Tel. (781) 857-1336

29
Freetown-Fall River State Forest
Freetown

Southeastern Massachusetts has a goldmine in these 60 miles of trails and 5,600 acres of woods. Most of the mountain biking comes in three flavors: motorcycle-made single-tracks, rock-strewn double-tracks, and well-drained gravel roads.

BACKGROUND:

Freetown-Fall River State Forest attracts a wide variety of visitors ranging from picnickers, hikers, and bikers to off-road motorcyclists and hunters, in season. Motorized trail usage is permitted in the warm season and the most active hunting period is late fall. Mountain biking is discouraged during deer season in November and December except on Sundays when hunting is prohibited by state law. On the other days at this time of year, all trail users are urged to take appropriate precautions and wear blaze orange clothing.

TRAIL POLICIES:

All trails and roads are currently open to mountain biking. Riders should note, however, that many of the single-tracks are severely eroded from motorcycle usage and are plagued by puddles, mudholes, and other drainage problems as a result. Keep to the network of gravel roads during mud season and other wet periods to avoid worsening this damage.

Gates to many of the gravel roads are left open so cars have access to places that you might not expect. Ride on the righthand side and be alert when using these routes.

All visitors are requested to avoid an area that is designated as the Wampanoag Indian Reservation, a spiritually sensitive area located southwest of the intersection of High St., Bell Rock Rd., and Copicut Rd.

Only the major lots are displayed on the map but parking is permitted at many points throughout the forest. Visitors are requested to use care in parking so as not to block access to trails in any way.

Generally, the terrain is milder in the eastern half of the forest and hillier in the west. In the east, the gravel roads allow easy cruising but the single-tracks are difficult because rocks, roots, and wet spots obstruct the way. In the west, the single-tracks enjoy smoother soils but encounter steep slopes that make them equally challenging.

Signs mark some of the gravel roads but none of the single-tracks. Visitors using the gravel roads can determine their location by noticing the numbers posted beside the forest's 31 water holes that were dug to assist fire fighters. These numbers appear on the accompanying map. Numbered intersections are also planned but were not established at the time of this printing.

Given the forest's remote location, large size, and array of trails, it is advisable to bring plenty of water, follow your course on a map, and ride with a companion.

Relatively smooth and well-drained, the 15 miles of gravel roads have easy biking conditions and can provide hours of scenic off-pavement exploration. They are also a good option for early season riding, especially since spring arrives a little earlier this far south.

Payne Road is a popular gateway to the forest's many options. It begins at Forest Headquarters on Slab Bridge Rd. and stretches for 1.3 miles to High St. with only one noticeable slope, a downhill, near the end. Payne Road intersects two other flat roads along the way, **Makepeace Road** which begins on the left within the first half-mile, and **Hathaway Road** which crosses after three quarters of a mile on a course that joins Makepeace with Slab Bridge Rd.

An easy, 6-mile loop on similar routes starts on Payne Road. Continue to the end at High St., turn left and ride on the pavement for 0.7 miles to a four-way intersection at **Copicut Road**, then turn left and follow it gradually uphill. The road crests near a granite post marking the border between Fall River and Freetown, then descends slightly and intersects **Cedar Swamp Road** after 1.4 miles. Turn left here and follow Cedar Swamp Road for 0.7 miles to its intersection with Makepeace Road, then turn left to return to Payne Road and complete the loop. Two lesser-traveled dirt roads, **Hathaway Extension** and the **Bent Rim Trail**, explore the area east of Makepeace Road and offer alternative routes back to Slab Bridge Rd. and the trailhead parking lot.

Ledge Road is the primary route through the western half of the forest. It runs for a half-mile from Bell Rock Rd., forks right at an intersection with Upper Ledge Road, then continues past the site of an abandoned quarry, now a granite-lined pool of water. A rougher ride, **Upper Ledge Road** descends to Rattlesnake Brook, turns sharply right, and begins a long climb that culminates with a grand view of the eastern horizon from the open ledge above the quarry. After this high point it drops back to Ledge Road and runs for another half-mile to the edge of Rte. 24. Combining Ledge and Upper Ledge roads makes a 3-mile loop from Bell Rock Rd.

DOUBLE-TRACKS:

The easiest double-track is the **railroad grade** that runs the short distance from Rte. 24 to the quarry site. Originally built to transport granite for the construction of Fall River's mill buildings, this grade has become an enjoyable trail with a smooth, flat surface. The parallel **Haskell Path** is another easy ride with mild hills and a stable surface.

Most other double-tracks require more effort from mountain bikers. Those near **Breakneck Hill** descend from Hathaway Road toward the railroad tracks on a slope that is rough in places but rideable. The trail paralleling the tracks at the bottom of this hill is flat and easy but dead ends at private property.

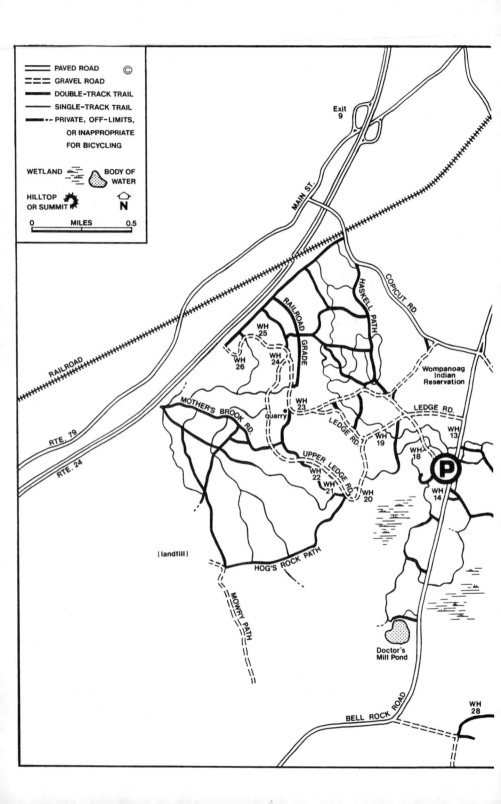

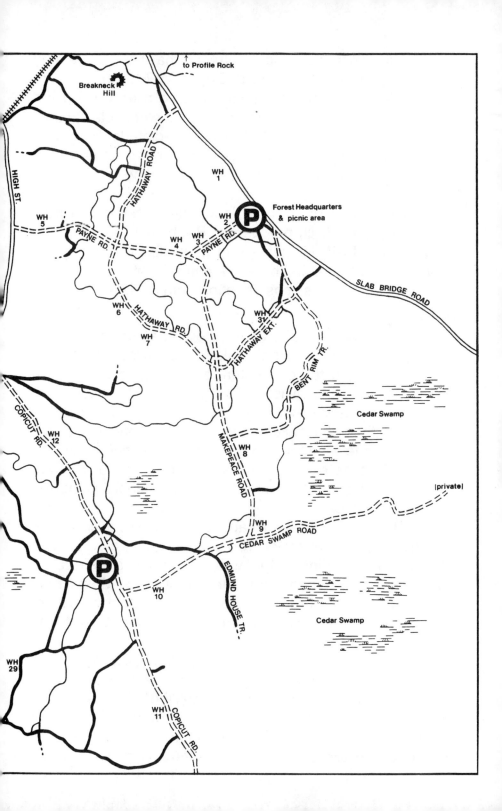

The two parallel double-tracks that link the parking lots on Bell Rock Rd. and Copicut Rd. range from intermediate to difficult with the northern trail being the roughest. Exposed rocks and numerous wet spots obstruct its surface. To the south, other intermediate-level double-tracks span longer distances between these roads in the area of water hole 28 with a rideable flow of hills and obstacles.

Mother's Brook Road is another rocky option from the high point on Upper Ledge Road to Rte. 24, while **Hog's Rock Path** is among the most difficult and meant only for expert riders. The trail's entire length is torn apart by rocks and requires constant effort from its riders.

SINGLE-TRACKS:

The single-tracks at Freetown-Fall River are the highlight for most mountain bikers. Created by off-road motorcycles and full of challenge, they generally earn a difficult rating as they twist and wrap through the woods with constant turns and dizzying appeal. Newcomers should be aware that their convoluted courses can be very disorienting and their nameless status makes any description inherently vague. Fortunately, most cross gravel roads or double-tracks at numerous locations to provide bail-out points for the weak and weary.

Those near Forest Headquarters lie in gentle terrain but are clogged by rocks, roots, and wet spots in many places, so the riding is tricky at best. The single-tracks spanning the distance from Copicut Road to Makepeace Road are among the forest's roughest with a multitude of wet areas and a mercilous flow of rocks giving little relief to pedalers.

The most exciting single-tracks lie west of Bell Rock Rd. where a combination of smoother soils and undulating terrain form an ideal off-road playground. Several paths leave directly from the Bell Rock Rd. parking lot south of Ledge Road. The area between Ledge Road and Haskell Path is especially recommended for its smooth turns, quick transitions, and hair-raising hills. Since motorcycles have been carving these trails for years, berms and banks have formed and allow extra control on the corners and dips, which is important when the trails cling to hillsides and sharp turns. Many of the uphills will prove to be simply too steep to pedal.

DRIVING DIRECTIONS:

To reach the Forest Headquarters parking lot, take Rte. 24 south to Exit 10 and follow North Main St. toward Assonet. At the village center 0.8 miles from Rte. 24, turn left on Rte. 79 north and then right after 0.1 miles on Elm St. This road becomes Slab Bridge Rd. and the parking lot is 1.8 miles ahead on the right.

To reach the Bell Rock Rd. parking lot, take Exit 9 from Rte. 24 and follow Rte. 79 north for 0.7 miles. Turn right on Hill St., which later becomes Bell Rock Rd., and the parking lot is 2.2 miles ahead on the right.

BIKE SHOPS:

Beauvais Bicycle, 181 Whittenton St., Taunton, Tel. (508) 824-5588

Crosby Cycle Company, 248 Tucker St., Fall River, Tel. (508) 679-9366

Fall River Bicycle, 769 Bedford St., Fall River, Tel. (508) 324-0466

Silver City Bicycles, Raynham Marketplace, 1470 Rte. 44, Raynham, Tel. (508) 828-9722

ADDITIONAL INFORMATION:

Freetown-Fall River State Forest, P.O. Box 171, Assonet, MA 02702, Tel. (508) 644-5522

30
Massasoit State Park
Taunton

The cluster of trails at Massasoit State Park offers surprisingly good riding whether you want an easy cruise on double-tracks or a challenging battle on single-tracks. Sandy soils keep the surfaces relatively smooth.

BACKGROUND:

Massasoit State Park is named in honor of a powerful Wompanoag Indian chief who lived in this area in the 1600's. Known for making treaties, Chief Massasoit negotiated with early settlers and was willing to sell large tracts of land, including what is now the park, in hopes of creating peace. This park was created in 1969 and encompasses over a thousand acres.

The 126-site campground is the park's predominant feature. It is open from early May to mid-October and fills to capacity during vacation periods, so call ahead to reserve your space. Hunting is permitted and is most popular from mid-October to mid-December.

TRAIL POLICIES:

Mountain biking is currently permitted on all trails at Massasoit State Park. Cyclists should be advised that sandy soils and steep slopes make trails vulnerable to erosion during wet periods, so do what you can to minimize your impact on the surface. Since several trails enter the campground and beach area, be as respectful as possible when riding through.

The entire length of Campground Road is open to car traffic from early May to mid-October, the camping season. During the remainder of the year, a gate blocks the road beyond the parking lot at the contact station, while a second gate that is located closer to Middleboro Ave. is locked at 3:30 PM each day. All cars must be out of the parking lot by this time. If you are planning to ride later than 3:30, park outside the outer gate.

The park's trails are not named or marked with signs but prominent features will help newcomers find their way. The most obvious is the pavement of Campground Road which leads from the main entrance gate to the center of the park, accessing the campground and intersecting much of the trail system along its 2-mile distance. Regardless of which trails you choose to ride, this road will never be far away.

In addition, four ponds dominate the park's landscape and will be helpful points of reference. The easiest trails for biking follow the shorelines of these ponds where the terrain is flatter while hillier options branch away from the water.

Generally, the double-tracks have easy conditions for biking and are found in the southern part of the park. For an easy, 3.2-mile introductory tour of the trails, begin at the parking lot at the contact station and head south on **Campground Road**. A short distance ahead at the road's first left-hand turn, bear right on a dirt road at a metal gate. Follow this trail across a bridge, up a sandy slope to a small clearing, then into the shade of woods, staying straight at two intersections along this distance. After a half-mile and just before the trail ends on Campground Road, turn right, cross a wet spot, and ride uphill to another intersection. Turn left here and continue past the Pudding Stone to the campground, then turn right and descend on a paved driveway to the beach area on **Middle Pond**. At the beach, turn right and begin circling Middle Pond in the counter-clockwise direction, turning left at all major intersections until you return to the end of Campground Road's pavement, 1.5 miles from the contact station.

Several adjoining trails offer extensions to this ride. Those that circle **Little Bearhole Pond** form a 1-mile loop

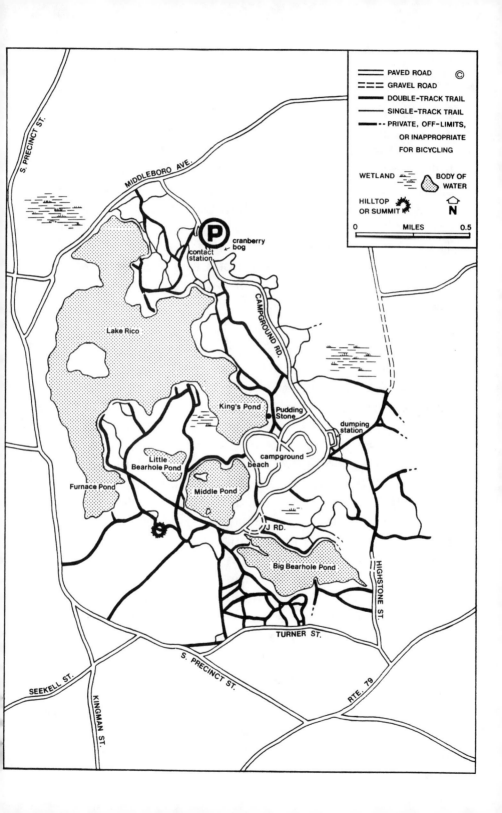

with some of the park's flattest, smoothest trail surfaces and worthwhile views over **Lake Rico**.

Trails running between Middle Pond and S. Precinct St. encounter hillier terrain and rougher surfaces but offer lots of solitude in one of the park's most remote corners.

Other mountain biking options include a cluster of trails south of **Big Bearhole Pond** off Turner St. but sandy conditions slow the riding at many points. **Highstone St.** extends along the park's eastern boundary and serves as a useful leg in a loop around Big Bearhole Pond. It begins on Turner St. as a public road and degrades to a trail as it passes the eastern tip of the pond and intersects two other double-tracks that return to Campground Road at the camper's dumping station.

SINGLE-TRACKS:

A small area of exciting single-tracks lies just west of the parking lot at the contact station. Branching from a few double-tracks in the area, these single-tracks wrap through hilly terrain above Lake Rico with intermediate and difficult conditions. The soils are relatively smooth but many of the slopes are steep.

Across Campground Road, an intermediate-level single-track tour leads riders from the contact station to Big Bearhole Pond over the course of about 2 miles, depending on the exact route taken. Begin just beyond the cranberry bog where a sign and footbridge guide the trail into the woods. The path climbs with several switchbacks up a small hill, descends the opposite side to the edge of Campground Road, and winds through the woods beside the road for much of the next 1.3 miles. The path splits at several points, with some options returning to the road and others penetrating deeper into the woods, but generally most continue in a southerly direction to the campround's dumping station.

Here the single-track route crosses two double-track trails and continues southward for another quarter-mile where it widens and ends with an abrupt climb. Turn right at this point on a trail that gradually narrows. After several descents, ascents, and lively turns, the trail emerges on a ridgeline above Big Bearhole Pond, a quarter-mile from **J Road** where a picnic area and view await on the shoreline.

DRIVING DIRECTIONS:

From Rte. 24 take Exit 13A and follow Rte. 44 east. Turn immediately right on Orchard St. (which becomes Colony Ave. in Taunton), and drive to the end at the village of East Taunton. Turn left here on Middleboro Ave. and find the park entrance 2 miles ahead on the right.

BIKE SHOPS:

Beauvais Bicycle Shop, 181 Whittenton St., Taunton, Tel. (508) 824-5588

Merle's Bike Shop, 201 W. Grove St., Middleboro, Tel. (508) 947-6232

Silver City Bicycles, Raynham Marketplace, 1470 Rte. 44, Raynham, Tel. (508) 828-9722

ADDITIONAL INFORMATION:

Massasoit State Park, Middleboro Ave., East Taunton, MA 02718, Tel. (508) 822-7405

31
Myles Standish State Forest
Carver

The Boston area's biggest mountain biking area lies 40 miles south of the city in the uniquely beautiful area of cranberry bogs and pine barrens of Carver and Plymouth. Sand slows the riding at some points but a vast range of options makes this 15,000-acre state forest and 100-mile trail network a true giant. 450 campsites await for those who plan ahead.

BACKGROUND:

The forest is New England's largest remaining *pine barren* ecosystem, a sandy environment where only low-growing pitch pines, scrub oaks, and other hardy plants can survive. Named for the military leader of Plymouth Colony, Myles Standish State Forest was established in 1916 in one of the first acts of a newly created State Forest Commission. At the time the land was considered of little value but its ponds and woodlands gradually became recognized as a recreational resource and in the early 1930's the Civilian Conservation Corps built bathhouses, beaches, picnic areas, campgrounds, and roads to suit growing numbers of visitors. The corps also planted stands of white and red pine that still shade the trails.

Campgrounds are the forest's main attraction in summer and are located at Fearing, Charge, Curlew, and Barrett ponds. Reservations are recommended. For day-trippers, swimming beaches are located at Fearing and College ponds. The nearly 15 miles of paved bike paths were built in the 1970's and reach a variety of destinations in the forest with relatively effortless riding while unpaved trails for mountain biking venture to more remote areas. One of the best times to mountain bike at Myles Standish is during winter when the trails' soft, sandy spots harden to become more rideable.

TRAIL POLICIES:

Mountain bikers should observe the standard rules of trail etiquette by riding in control, signaling your approach to other trail users to avoid startling them, and sharing the trail. Do not ride on trails that are posted as being closed to bikes.

Hunting is a permitted and popular activity at Myles Standish. For reasons of safety, all recreational trails are closed on Saturdays and holidays from mid-October to early January and all of deer week of the shotgun season each year. Hunting seasons and regulations are posted at many trailheads. Hunting is prohibited by state law on Sundays.

ORIENTATION:

When planning any trail excursion at Myles Standish, realize that this state forest is the size of an average town in the Boston area. A grid-like network of fire roads divides the property into blocks that range from a half-mile to a mile in size. Signs display the road names at most intersections but none are present to mark the tangle of single-track trails. Other landmarks that are useful in finding your way include paved roads, paved bike paths, electric powerlines, and gas pipelines.

GRAVEL ROADS:

The gravel roads are relatively straight but this should not suggest that the terrain is flat, as a steady supply of hills makes many of these roads a demanding ride for bikers. Pockets of deep sand, typically at the bottoms of hills where rain has washed it down the slope, mire bicycle tires and often require walking. Try to avoid any route along a **gas pipeline** or **powerline** corridor because these are especially plagued by loose sand and devoid of interesting scenery.

East Line Road is a 4-mile ride along the forest's eastern boundary with hills and sandy spots slowing the trip. On the opposite boundary, 3.5-mile **West Line Road** has similar conditions with slightly better scenery and a curvier, shadier course. Joining the two, **Three Cornered Pond Road** spans the width of the state forest over nearly 5 miles

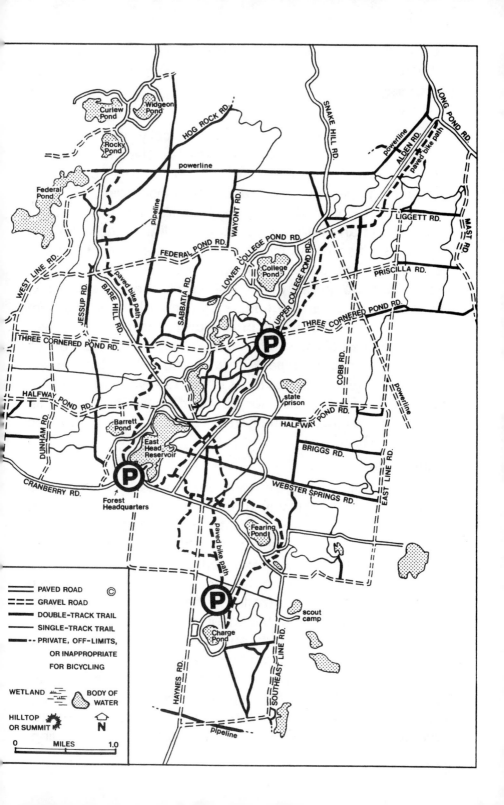

Curlew Pond
Widgeon Pond
Rocky Pond
HOG ROCK RD.
SNAKE HILL RD.
LONG POND RD.
powerline
ALDEN RD.
paved bike path
Federal Pond
Pipeline
powerline
LIGGETT RD.
MAST RD.
WAYONT RD.
FEDERAL POND RD.
LOWER COLLEGE POND RD.
College Pond
UPPER COLLEGE POND RD.
PRISCILLA RD.
WEST LINE RD.
JESSUP RD.
paved bike path
BARE HILL RD.
SABBATIA RD.
THREE CORNERED POND RD.
P
THREE CORNERED POND RD.
COBB RD.
powerline
HALFWAY POND RD.
DUNHAM RD.
Barrett Pond
East Head Reservoir
state prison
HALFWAY POND RD.
BRIGGS RD.
EAST LINE RD.
CRANBERRY RD.
P
Forest Headquarters
WEBSTER SPRINGS RD.
paved bike path
Fearing Pond
PAVED ROAD   ©
GRAVEL ROAD
DOUBLE-TRACK TRAIL
SINGLE-TRACK TRAIL
PRIVATE, OFF-LIMITS,
  OR INAPPROPRIATE
  FOR BICYCLING

WETLAND
BODY OF WATER

HILLTOP
OR SUMMIT
N

P
scout camp
Charge Pond
HAYNES RD.
SOUTHEAST LINE RD.

0   MILES   1.0
Pipeline

passing a variety of surroundings and many intersecting options.

DOUBLE-TRACKS:

Barely distinguishable from the gravel roads in places, Myles Standish's double-tracks are typically narrower, less-traveled versions of the same fire roads. Their surfaces are typically firmer and covered with the fallen needles of surrounding trees, although sandy spots also exist.

Avoid **Kamesit Way**, which shares the gas pipeline corridor, and any trails along the **powerlines** since they get regular use by off-road motorcycles and are loose with sand as a result. The collection of east-west double-tracks along the eastern boundary offers rolling hills and few signs of civilization, and can be linked with gravel roads that run north-south. **Webster Springs Road**, one of the longest, passes a series of mowed fields near its eastern end that are maintained for bird habitat. To the north, **Hog Rock Road** climbs at a faint pitch for most of its 1.8-mile length until it reaches the forest's northern border where the trail turns southward, narrows to single-track, and returns for 1.5 miles to **Wayout Road**.

SINGLE-TRACKS:

Most of the single-tracks were made by motorcycles so they take wild, curvey routes through the woods that range from intermediate to difficult. Some of the best lie in a tight cluster located between the trailhead parking lots at the center of the state forest where firm surfaces and plenty of sharp corners make for great mountain biking. Note that hikers also use these trails so be ready to yield trail. Newcomers will surely be disoriented by the maze of narrow pathways but paved roads surround the network and the area is not remote. Blue tree tags mark most of the trails.

The 2.7-mile loop around **East Head Reservoir** is an especially scenic ride. Starting at the headquarters parking lot, the trail follows the shoreline with a smooth, needle-covered treadway and few hills, making it fairly easy riding.

The loop joins the pavement of a road for a short distance at one point and the soft sand of a pipeline at another but is otherwise deep in the shade of woods.

Look to the eastern side of the forest for another ten or so miles of good single-tracks. Here lively hills, carved corners, and the narrow confines of the trail provide a vast difference from the nearby fire roads. Note that these trails explore remote sections of the state forest and some run for a mile before reaching their next intersection so it is important to follow the map closely. Intersecting fire roads provide plenty of bail-out points.

DRIVING DIRECTIONS:

From I-495 take Exit 2 and follow Rte. 58 north for 2.5 miles. Where Rte. 58 turns left, continue straight on Tremont St. and drive for another 0.7 miles. Turn right on Cranberry Rd. and follow it to the end at Forest Headquarters.

From Rte. 3 take Exit 5 and follow Long Pond Rd. south for 3.7 miles to the Alden Rd. entrance on the right. Drive for 1.5 miles to a four-way intersection. Either turn left and follow Upper College Pond Rd. for 1.2 miles to a parking lot on the right or stay straight and follow Lower College Pond Rd. to the end at Forest Headquarters, on the left.

BIKE SHOPS:

Cycleville, 2228 State Rd. (Rte 3A), Plymouth, Tel. (508) 888-5160

Martha's Bicycles, 300 Court St. (Rte 3A), Plymouth, Tel. (508) 746-2109

Serious Cycles, 265 State Rd. (Rte 3A), Plymouth, Tel. (508) 746-2756

ADDITIONAL INFORMATION:

Myles Standish State Forest, Cranberry Rd., P.O. Box 66, S. Carver, MA 02366, Tel. (508) 866-2526

campground reservations: (877) 422-6762

32
Duxbury Conservation Lands
Duxbury

The mountain biking at Duxbury is smooth and scenic. Few rocks disrupt the trail surfaces and fallen pine needles form a welcome cushion on the ground, leaving pedalers free to focus their attention on the distinctive scenery of cranberry bogs, ponds, and deep forests. Riding conditions are mostly easy and intermediate.

BACKGROUND:

This natural preserve is a collection of different properties totaling nearly 1,000 acres and managed by various branches of town government and private conservation groups. A portion of the acreage is designated as public water supply land and another is a wildlife sanctuary of the Massachusetts Audubon Society, managed for the protection of nesting birds and other wildlife.

Other areas of the land are devoted to growing cranberries, an important crop for Duxbury. In hopes of preserving this agricultural heritage the town has acquired many of its cranberry bogs and leases them to local growers, producing an array of open spaces that add a unique flavor to the scenery. Visitors are welcome to use the dirt roads and trails surrounding these bogs but should stay clear of the crops, irrigation ditches, and equipment. Harvesting occurs during the early fall when trucks and equipment will be using the access roads.

A color map delineating all of the town's open spaces is for sale at Duxbury Town Offices. A contribution box at the trailhead infromation kiosk makes it possible for visitors to show their support for the maintenance of the trails by leaving a donation.

TRAIL POLICIES:

Regulations posted at the trailhead call for passive

uses only. Since much of this area is a designated wildlife sanctuary, be respectful of the surrounding environment by riding quietly, at a safe speed, and only when conditions are dry. Remain on the trails and remember to check trailhead bulletin boards for policy changes.

Hunting and the use of motorized vehicles are not permitted and the area is open only during daylight hours.

ORIENTATION:

Two small parking lots, on opposite sides of Mayflower St., are located at the center of the trail network. A cluster of mostly easy double-tracks awaits south of the road while a larger number of options lie to the north including double-tracks that are generally easy riding and single-tracks that are intermediate or difficult.

Most trails are not named and signs of any kind are not posted, with the exception of a short series of numbered intersections south of Mayflower St. Look for the various bodies of water, cranberry bogs, and hills to be helpful landmarks as you explore the area.

DOUBLE-TRACKS:

South of Mayflower St., the 1.7-mile **Yellow-Blazed Trail** originates at the parking lot and follows a series of numbered intersections through an area of water views and broad cranberry bogs with mostly easy biking conditions. The route follows a woods road downhill to Round Pond bearing left at intersections 1 and 2, climbs a small hill past several other intersections, then descends to intersection 3 near Pine Lake where it turns right. At intersection 4 it bears left on a short, bumpy path beside Round Pond that can easily be walked. It then emerges beside a pumphouse, crosses a footbridge, and follows a dike that separates the pond from the Loring Cranberry Bogs. The Yellow-Blazed Trail rises into the woods at the northern end of the bogs, bends right at intersection 5, and soon ends at Mayflower St. a short distance west of the parking lot.

Quiet double-tracks branch southward from this point.

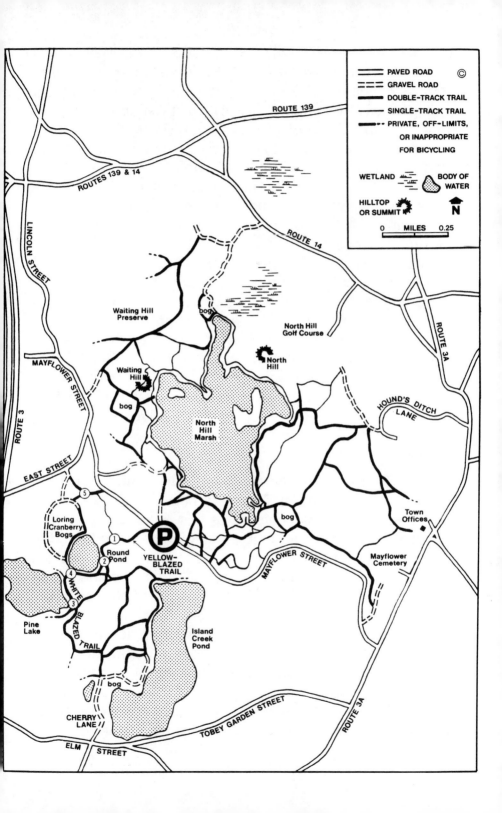

The **White-Blazed Trail**, also marked as the Bay Circuit Trail, a route planned to eventually circle the Boston area from Newburyport to Duxbury, continues from intersection 3 with gentle conditions to Cherry La. The unnamed trail following the edge of Island Creek Pond and another cranberry bog is an easy ride also. Beware the steep, eroded trail that links the northern end of Island Creek Pond with the Yellow-Blazed Trail near intersection 2, since loose rocks make it a struggle to ride in either direction.

North of Mayflower St., more double-tracks explore the surroundings of **North Hill Marsh**, a wildlife sanctuary. On the western side it is possible to follow a combination of easy woods roads northward as far as Rte. 14, while on the eastern side double-tracks stretch to the Town Offices on Rte. 3A. A number of kettleholes, huge basins in the ground formed by the melting of blocks of glacial ice thousands of years ago, can be seen in the area east of the marsh. For the best view over the marsh itself, continue past the metal gate at the parking lot and follow the trail to the first intersection, turn right, then look for a wooden viewing platform ahead on the left.

SINGLE-TRACKS:

A 3-mile, intermediate-level tour around North Hill Marsh captures some of Duxbury's best single-track riding. Note that several low spots make this route a poor choice during wet periods. From the parking lot head north up the main trail, take the first right on a trail leading to the water's edge, then turn left and follow the western side of the marsh on a course spiced with fallen trees and tight corners. Hills are few so the pedaling is manageable.

After a mile the route traverses a hillside above the water, emerges beside a cranberry bog at the marsh's northern reach, then turns right and returns southward on the opposite shore. Skirting the edge of the town's North Hill Golf Course at one point, it soon reverts to a woodland path weaving through trees until it scrambles up a final slope and ends at a woods road. Turn right and follow this rolling double-track along the water to its terminus, then turn right again on a path that circles the southern tip of the marsh and ends at a double-track that is blazed in yellow. Turn left to reach Mayflower St., just east of the parking lot.

Several other single-tracks are worth exploring near this endpoint. Narrow and curvey, they roam through an area of small hills with intermediate and difficult conditions.

DRIVING DIRECTIONS:

From Rte. 3 take Exit 11 and follow Rte. 14 east toward Duxbury center. Turn immediately right on Lincoln St. and drive for 0.7 miles to where it joins Mayflower St. Continuing straight on Mayflower St., bear left at the next fork (where East St. branches to the right), and look for trailhead parking areas 0.5 miles ahead on both sides of the road.

BIKE SHOPS:

Bicycle Junction, 94 Washington St. (Rte. 53), Pembroke, Tel. (781) 826-6385

Bikeway, Marshfield Plaza, Marshfield, Tel. (781) 837-2453

Country Ski & Bike, 901 Winter St., Hanson, Tel. (781) 826-2022

Martha's Bicycles, 300 Court St. (Rte. 3A), Plymouth, Tel. (781) 746-2109

Ski Market, Rte. 139, Pembroke, Tel. (781) 826-1155

ADDITIONAL INFORMATION:

Bay Circuit Alliance, 3 Railroad St., Andover, MA 01810, Tel. (978) 470-1982

Duxbury Conservation Commission, Duxbury Town Offices, Duxbury, MA 02331

Massachusetts Audubon Society, S. Great Rd., Lincoln, MA 01773, Tel. (781) 259-9500

33
Carolina Hill Reservation
Marshfield

Cooled by ocean breezes, the gravelly hills of Marshfield hold a 15-mile treasure of paths and old wagon roads that are perfect for mountain biking. A few trails are either easy or difficult but the majority have intermediate-level conditions.

BACKGROUND:

Hilly terrain and sandy, arid soil made this land undesireable for farming in Marshfield's early days and spared it from much development. Old roads and trails, named in the 1700's for the families whose homes they served, are among the few signs of any human activity. Now owned by the town, the land is preserved in a natural state and much of it is designated as watershed property for the public water supply.

TRAIL POLICIES:

Passive recreation is welcome at the Carolina Hill Reservation. Mountain bikers are advised to be sensitive to erosion since the property's hilly terrain and sandy soils leave trail surfaces vulnerable, especially during rainy periods. Washouts already plague some trails and cyclists are urged to pedal softly, avoid skidding, and avoid riding when the ground is wet.

Although motorized vehicles are prohibited, it is clear that they frequent the trails and contribute to much of the erosion problem. Hunting is not permitted and the area is open from dawn to dusk.

ORIENTATION:

The parking lot lies at the eastern edge of the reservation. Heading west, trails lead uphill to high points at the center of the reservation and, continuing westward, descend to a stream valley that runs along the western edge of the trail system.

A few old roads and trails retain their colonial-era names but signs are not present at intersections to display them. The surrounding network of paved roads will provide help in plotting your position, as will numbers that are painted on gates at certain road/trail intersections. These gate numbers are displayed on the accompanying map so bring it along if you are exploring the area for the first time.

DOUBLE-TRACKS:

Some of the area's flattest mountain biking extends directly north and south from the parking lot along an abandoned **railroad bed**. Once a segment of the Duxbury and Cohasset Railroad, this line operated from 1867 to 1939 and has been reborn as a popular recreation trail that stretches for 3 miles through the heart of town. Although its rails and ties have been removed, the grade is an arduous ride in a few spots where its surface has loose sand. Heading south, the trail overlaps a driveway for a short distance, crosses Clay Pit Rd. after a half-mile, and passes several intersecting motorcycle paths before reaching South River St. at 1.5 miles. Grass carpets the final, quarter-mile stretch to the site of a missing bridge over the South River where a view spreads over a broad marshland.

To the north, the railroad bed departs from gate 12 on a 2-mile run to Station St. (Note that a private driveway forks left beside this gate.) Starting with a wide, gravel surface, the trail gradually narrows as it approaches Pinehurst Rd. and gains a quieter, grassy surface.

Eames Way is another easy option for biking, but it also suffers from loose sand in a few spots. Both ends of this old road are paved and open to cars but its midsection is closed to traffic for the 1.2 miles between gate 1 and gate 8. This distance is characterized by a wide gravel surface and a gentle slope that approaches the reservation's highest elevations. To complete an easy, 6-mile loop from the parking lot using a combination of trails and local roads, follow the railroad bed north to Station St., turn left and then

224

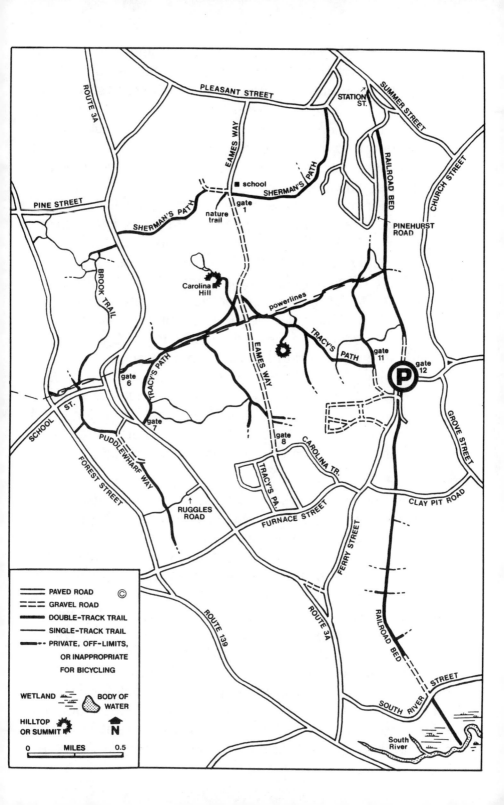

left again on Summer St. After a short distance turn left on Pleasant St. and ride for 0.6 miles, then turn left on Eames Way and ride through the reservation to the road's endpoint at the bottom of a hill. Turn left on Furnace St., left on Ferry St., then immediately right on Clay Pit Rd. Look for the railroad bed less than a quarter-mile ahead on the left, just before a sand pit area on the right, and follow it northward back to the parking lot.

Other double-tracks intersect this loop with varying conditions. The 1.4-mile **Sherman's Path** has intermediate conditions on both ends where moderate slopes and exposed rocks are present, but its midsection is an easy ride. Both **Tracy's Path** and the adjoining road along the **powerlines** tackle some steeper slopes where erosion has left loose rocks that make the mountain biking difficult.

Side trails reach the tree-covered top of **Carolina Hill** as well as a neighboring hill that offers an ocean vista. To find this view, follow Tracy's Path from Eames Way toward the parking lot. After forking to the right from the powerlines and entering the woods, take the first right on a dead end double-track that climbs abruptly to the top of a small knob where surrounding trees have been cleared to allow a view.

SINGLE-TRACKS:

Single-tracks are limited but segments of trail exist throughout the reservation. For a difficult ride, try the one that begins near Eames Way at gate 8 and descends to the end of Tracy's Path at gate 7. Although the surface is fairly smooth, a hedge of low bushes defines a narrow width to the trail for most of the way and steep terrain warrants caution. It starts with a brief hill climb, then flattens with a swerving course through the woods, and finishes with a straight, steep drop where erosion has taken its toll.

Cross Rte. 3A to find more single-track riding. Turn left at the end of Tracy's Path at gate 7 and look for Ruggles Rd. less than a half-mile ahead on the right. A footpath leads from the end of this dead end street to more conservation land and trails for mountain biking in the valley of Furnace Brook. In a short distance it intersects **Puddlewharf Way**, an easy ride and primary trail through the area. Puddlewharf Way heads to the right (north) and enters the openness of a former sandpit following its righthand (eastern) edge for a half-mile. Many other tracks diverge along this distance to explore various parts of the sandpit but bicyclists are advised to stay on this main route where traction is best. It joins a dirt road for part of this short distance and, where this road turns to the right and becomes paved, Puddlewharf Way continues straight and soon reenters the woods. The trail bumps over tree roots in the shade of forest for the last third of a mile to School St.

Cross School St. and continue to the powerlines, turn right and then immediately left on the **Brook Trail**. An intermediate-level single-track, this path is flat for much of the way but encounters three noticeable hills and lots of logs, wet spots, and tree roots in between. Its 2.4-mile course ends at Pine St. and intersects several other trails, some that end on private property.

DRIVING DIRECTIONS:
From Rte. 3 take Exit 12 and follow Rte. 139 east for 2.8 miles. Turn left on Rte. 3A north and continue for 0.6 miles, then bear right at a fork on Ferry St. The trailhead, marked by a green, metal gate at a gravel turn-out, is 1.2 miles ahead on the left after a sharp, right-hand turn. Be careful not to block either the gate or a private driveway that lead from this parking area.

BIKE SHOPS:
Bicycle Junction, 94 Washington St. (Rte. 53), Pembroke, Tel. (781) 826-6385
Bikeway, Marshfield Plaza, Marshfield, Tel. (781) 837-2453
Cycle Lodge, 1269 Washington St. (Rte. 53), Hanover, Tel. (781) 829-9197
Ski Market, Rte. 139, Pembroke, Tel. (781) 826-1155

ADDITIONAL INFORMATION:
Marshfield Conservation Commission, 870 Morain St., Marshfield, MA 02050

34

Wompatuck State Park
Hingham

Wompatuck is a bicycle playground. Its popular network of paved bike paths has provided family fun for over two decades and now a much larger collection of great single-tracks keeps mountain bikers coming back for more.

BACKGROUND:

This state park owes its origin to the U.S. Navy which occupied the property during World War II and established it as the country's primary ammunition storage facility for North Atlantic forces. In 1966 the state of Massachusetts acquired most of the land for use as a park and transformed many of the roads and railroad grades into a network of paved bike paths. Remains of the underground bunkers are still evident and the old chainlink fence that guarded the munitions now marks the park boundary.

Wompatuck also offers a campground from mid-April to mid-October for those who want to spend the night. Reservations are recommended.

The New England Mountain Bike Association's Southeast Mass. chapter has been hard at work on Wompatuck's trails, assisting the park's staff in building bridges and boardwalks, rerouting eroded trails to more sustainable locations, and creating new single-tracks. If you would like to join the fun, contact NEMBA.

TRAIL POLICIES:

Mountain biking is permitted on all official trails within the park. Riders are requested to announce their presence to avoid startling other trail users and to travel at safe speeds. Because the paved bike routes intersect the mountain biking trails at many points, watch for other cyclists when emerging on the pavement.

All visitors should be aware that the gate at the main

entrance is locked each night. The closing time varies through the year according to day length so note it when you enter and be sure to leave on time.

ORIENTATION:

Wompatuck is a huge area with a labyrinth of unmarked and unnamed roads and trails, which makes getting lost relatively easy. Maps are stationed at points throughout the park but it will be helpful to bring a map with you and follow your progress carefully. The accompanying map incorporates data obtained from the Department of Environmental Management's global positioning system.

The park is divided in half by the dead-end pavement of Union St., which is open to cars. Aside from the campground, all other paved roads are closed to motorized travel. Other helpful landmarks include the campground, Aaron Reservoir at the eastern boundary, and the chainlink fence that surrounds the entire park.

DOUBLE-TRACKS:

Starting at the main entrance gate, the **Woodpecker Trail** has a smooth, straight surface as it travels the boundary fence for a half-mile to Woodpecker Pond. A hill climb demands some energy but the route's finish of processed stone eliminates any other difficulties. Beyond the pond the trail turns between trees and exposed rocks but the riding remains generally easy. A NEMBA boardwalk bridges a wet area at the endpoint.

A string of other double-tracks spreads southward for several miles from the visitor center to Prospect St. with a range of easy and intermediate conditions. Areas of rocks, roots, or wet spots slow the riding along some portions but other sections remain smooth. The short spur that ascends Prospect Hill, Hingham's highest point, is both steep and eroded so it is a difficult ride.

Easy and intermediate-level double-tracks lie on both ends of Aaron Reservoir and offer short loops of a mile or so, with good scenery along the way. The designated

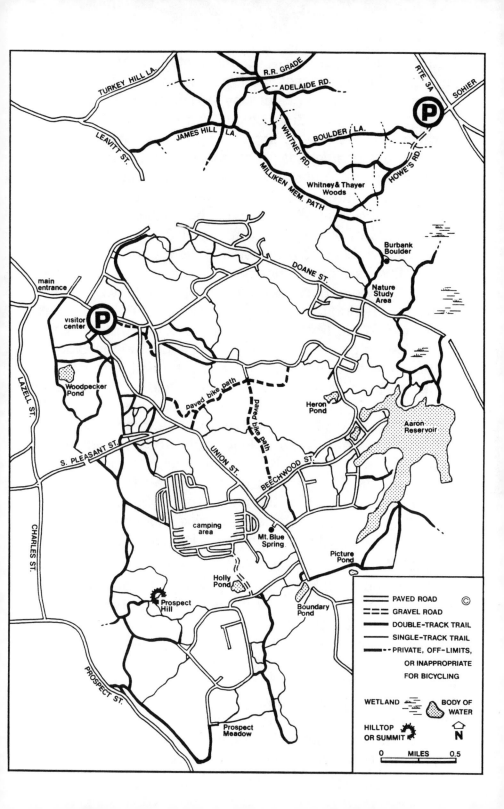

Nature Study Area has a 1.2-mile, intermediate-level loop off Doane St. that passes the Burbank Boulder, a huge rock left perched on a slab of ledge by the last glacier.

Beyond the Nature Study Area is beautiful **Whitney and Thayer Woods**, a separate property owned by the Trustees of Reservations. Mountain biking is permitted only on double-track routes at this reservation and cyclists are requested to ride in a safe manner, yield to others, and remain on existing trails. Mountain biking is prohibited each spring between March 1 and April 30 to protect trail surfaces. Regulations are posted at the Rte. 3A trailhead.

Howe's Road connects Wompatuck to this parking lot with a smooth, gravelly finish for much of the way. It also forms the first leg of an easy, 3.7-mile tour. Follow Howe's Road toward the trailhead, then turn left on **Boulder Lane** and follow its gently rolling course past the 200-ton Bigelow Boulder, Cohasset's biggest rock. At the end, turn right on **Whitney Road**, then left on **Adelaide Road** and descend to an old railroad grade. Turn left and follow this even grade for 0.4 miles and turn left at the next double-track intersection, where **James Hill Lane** crosses. Returning eastward, this trail rises over a small hill to an intersection where Ayer's Lane enters on the left and the **Milliken Memorial Path** starts on the right. Turn right and follow the Milliken for 0.8 miles past overhanging rhododendrons and some of the area's finest scenery back to Howe's Road.

SINGLE-TRACKS:

Wompatuck's large and growing network of single-tracks is the draw for many riders. Miles of these narrow, curvey paths unfold in a marathon of intermediate and difficult mountain biking that is tamed by plenty of bail-out points on intersecting paved roads. Sharp eyes will notice that a well-worn, marked route for mountain biking links many of the best paths and is identifiable by the letters *MB* and an arrow painted on the pavement at road intersections.

Since Wompatuck's single-tracks remain unnamed, any descriptions are inherently vague but conditions can be summarized for several parts of the park. Some of the newest and best options await in a cluster located northeast of the visitor center where small hills, tight spaces, and just the right number of obstacles add life to the biking. A smaller group off S. Pleasant St attracts a steady following eager to play in an abrupt terrain of sharp drops and turns.

The single-tracks near Aaron Reservoir's western shore are among the park's roughest but they are still rideable for skilled pedalers. To the south, those near Prospect Meadow are a bit milder but expect to steer past a steady flow of rocks and roots. Climbing Prospect Hill is possible from several directions and, although the incline is steep and broken with rocks, the paths allow room for wheels to roll. Trees block the view from the top.

DRIVING DIRECTIONS:

From Rte. 3 take Exit 14 and follow signs for Rte. 228 north. After 3.6 miles turn right on Free St. and the main entrance is 0.8 miles ahead on the right. Park at the visitor center.

To reach the Whitney & Thayer Woods trailhead, drive 6.5 miles from Rte. 3 on Rte. 228. Turn right on Rte. 3A and drive south for 2 miles, then look for a small sign for the Trustees of Reservations on the right, opposite Sohier St.

BIKE SHOPS:

Bicycle Clinic, 79 Pleasant St., S. Weymouth, Tel. (781) 340-1212

Bicycle Link, 230 Washington St. (Rte. 53), Weymouth, Tel. (781) 337-7125

Cohasset Cycle Sports, 754 Chief Justice Cushing Hwy. (Rte. 3A), Cohasset, Tel. (781) 383-0707

Cycle Lodge, 1269 Washington St. (Rte. 53), Hanover, Tel. (781) 829-9197

Western Performance Cyclery, 213 Washington St. (Rte. 53), Weymouth, Tel. (781) 337-1849

ADDITIONAL INFORMATION:

Wompatuck State Park, Union St., Hingham, MA 02043, Tel. (781) 749-7160

The Trustees of Reservations, 572 Essex St., Beverly, MA 01915, Tel. (978) 921-1944

NEMBA, (800) 57-NEMBA or web: www.nemba.org

35
World's End Reservation
Hingham

Some of the Boston area's prettiest mountain biking is at World's End Reservation, a peninsula where tree-lined trails roll gracefully through a landscape of hillside fields and ocean views. Not the place for a fast-paced workout or an extended tour, the reservation's 8 miles of trails are a haven for easy biking and suited for all ages and abilities.

BACKGROUND:

Since 1967 World's End has been the property of the Trustees of Reservations, a private land conservation group dedicated to preserving natural and historic places in Massachusetts. In earlier years, the land had been farmed as part of the estate of the Brewers, a wealthy family from Boston, and in the 1890's it was destined to become a planned community of 150 homes. The network of carriage roads and many rows of trees were established at this time under plans of Frederick Law Olmstead, the renowned landscape architect who designed Boston's Franklin Park and New York's Central Park. Fortunately the development never materialized and the land is now preserved as another "Olmsted park."

World's End Reservation is a well-kept place. Trails are carefully tended, water bars have been dug to prevent erosion, benches wait at viewpoints, and the acres of hay fields are cut several times each year to maintain the open landscape. The trailhead has toilet facilities and a staffed ranger station for information and trail maps. A small admission fee is charged to support these efforts.

TRAIL POLICIES:

Bicycles are permitted on all trails at the reservation. The idyllic scenery lends peace to the riding but draws large numbers of visitors to the trails, so pedal carefully. The staff asks bicyclists to ride slowly, yield to others, and remain on the trails. Riding across the fields is not permitted. The many walkers, dogs, kids, and others enjoying the area on sunny weekend days will appreciate not being surprised by your sudden appearance, so give a friendly greeting as you approach.

ORIENTATION:

Although trail signs are not present, the reservation's peninsular location makes it difficult to become lost and the open landscape and distinctive topography assist newcomers in finding their way. Easy double-track trails spread northward from the ranger station past four hills before reaching the end of the peninsula, and hold few surprises. Expect to find plenty of trail width, gradual slopes, and smooth surfaces of either grass or processed stone. The single-tracks are typically intermediate riding.

DOUBLE-TRACKS:

Brewer Road begins at the ranger station and ventures into the reservation with a surface of crushed stone. It dips to a pond and marshland where it is possible to observe swans and other bird life, then rises through a wide hay field on the gradual slope of **Pine Hill**. A drumlin, this and neighboring hills were formed during the Ice Age and consist largely of till, a mixture of clay, gravel, and rock. Drumlins are typically found in clusters with their rounded, elliptical shapes oriented in the direction of glacial flow, as the surrounding hills are. Arcing to the right, the road then crests with a vista over Hingham Harbor and the first view of the Boston skyline.

Brewer Road descends briefly before starting a second incline at the foot of **Planter's Hill**, bearing left at the next fork. A grass trail that continues straight at this intersection climbs to the top of the hill, the highest point at the reservation measuring 120 feet above sea level. Since the ocean lies only about 500 feet away, this side trip offers a worth-while view. A stone monument marks the top with

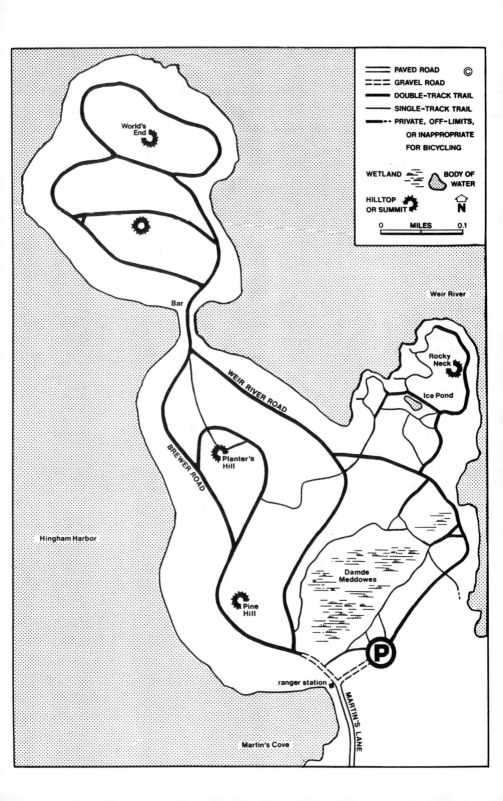

World's End

Weir River

Rocky Neck

Ice Pond

Bar

WEIR RIVER ROAD

BREWER ROAD

Planter's Hill

Hingham Harbor

Damde Meddowes

Pine Hill

P

ranger station

MARTIN'S LANE

Martin's Cove

PAVED ROAD   ©
GRAVEL ROAD
DOUBLE-TRACK TRAIL
SINGLE-TRACK TRAIL
PRIVATE, OFF-LIMITS,
OR INAPPROPRIATE
FOR BICYCLING

WETLAND   BODY OF WATER

HILLTOP OR SUMMIT   N

0   MILES   0.1

the grave of Arthur Edwards who spent most of his life working the surrounding land.

Brewer Road continues around the western side of Planter's Hill and after three quarters of a mile reaches the **bar**, a stone causeway built in the 1700's to link the peninsula's outermost land. Sea water borders each side of this earthen bridge and the salty air breezes are easily noticed. Grassy **Weir River Road** joins on the right at this point and extends on a mostly flat, 0.7-mile course around the eastern side of Planter's Hill back to the ranger station with a variety of shade trees lining the way.

Crossing the bar, the main flow of traffic continues to the right of an unnamed hill and follows the eastern edge of the peninsula, passing two trails on the left and then descending to a final intersection in a tree-covered valley. Turn hard right at this point and continue northward along the shore. Fewer people visit this outer part of the reservation so the trail has a grassy surface and a quieter feel. A wooden bench marks the peninsula's northern reach at **World's End**, 1.5 miles from the parking lot, where the trail bends around the hill and returns to the south.

Some intermediate riding conditions exist in the area of **Rocky Neck** where narrower trails and bumpier surfaces at a few points add more challenge for bicyclists. Rocky Neck is directly accessed by an easy double-track that continues straight from the end of the parking lot. After a half-mile of flat terrain, turn right at a row of planted trees and continue for another half-mile of easy riding over small hills along the eastern shore of the reservation. Pretty scenes of the **Weir River** appear at several places. The double-track width ends at the point of land where the trail encounters exposed ledge and becomes rougher. Ice Pond sits in a valley along this route and was once a sourse of ice, but it is now overgrown and difficult to notice.

Those who want to test their agility riding single-tracks have only a few choices at World's End. The western side of Rocky Neck has a trail that clings to slopes and ledges above the water with some excellent views across to the World's End peninsula. Closer to the parking lot, several paths trace the edge of a wetland with narrow courses that are bumpy with roots. Remember that hikers frequent these trails so ride at a safe speed and be ready to yield.

DRIVING DIRECTIONS:

From Rte. 3 take Exit 14 and follow Rte. 228 north for 5.8 miles. Turn left on Kilby St., located 6 tenths of a mile beyond Hingham Town Offices, then immediately left on Summer St. Continue for a half-mile, crossing Rte. 3A and reaching a traffic signal on Rockland St. Continue straight at this intersection onto Martin's Lane and the reservation is at the end, 0.7 miles ahead.

BIKE SHOPS:

Bicycle Clinic, 79 Pleasant St., S. Weymouth, Tel. (781) 340-1212

Bicycle Link, 230 Washington St. (Rte. 53), Weymouth, Tel. (781) 337-7125

Cohasset Cycle Sports, 754 Chief Justice Cushing Hwy., (Rte. 3A), Cohasset, Tel. (781) 383-0707

Western Performance Cyclery, 213 Washington St. (Rte. 3A), Weymouth, Tel. (781) 337-1849

ADDITIONAL INFORMATION:

World's End Reservation, Tel. (781) 749-8956

The Trustees of Reservations, 572 Essex St., Beverly, MA 01915, Tel. (978) 921-1944

Appendix

List of Organizations

Appalachian Mountain Club, 5 Joy St., Boston, MA 02108, Tel. (617) 523-0636,
web: www.outdoors.org

Bay Circuit Alliance, 3 Railroad St., Andover, MA 01810, Tel. (978) 470-1982

Essex County Greenbelt Association, 82 Eastern Ave., Essex, MA 01929, Tel. (978) 768-7241

International Mountain Bike Association, P.O. Box 7578, Boulder, CO 80306, Tel. (303) 545-9011,
web: http://www.imba.com

Massachusetts Audubon Society, South Great Rd., Lincoln, MA 01773, Tel. (781) 259-9500,
web: www.massaudubon.org

Massachusetts Department of Environmental Management, Division of Forests and Parks, 100 Cambridge St., 19'th Floor, Boston, MA 02202, Tel. (617) 727-3180
web: www.state.ma.us/dem

Massachusetts Department of Fisheries and Wildlife, P.O. Box 86, Acton, MA 01720, Tel. (978) 263-4347
web: www.state.ma.us/dfwele/dfw

MassBike, 44 Bromfield St. #207, Boston, MA 02108, Tel. (617) 542-BIKE,
web: http://www.massbike.org

Metropolitan District Commission, 20 Somerset St., Boston, MA 02108, Tel. (617) 727-1300, web: www.state.ma.us/mdc

New England Mountain Bike Association, P.O. Box 2221, Acton, MA 01720, Tel. (800) 57-NEMBA, web: www.nemba.org

Rails-to-Trails Conservancy, 1100 Seventeenth St. NW, 10'th Floor, Washington, DC 20036, Tel. (202) 331-9696, web: www.railtrails.org

The Trust for Public Land, 33 Union St., 4'th Floor, Boston, MA 02108, Tel. (617) 367-6200, web: www.tpl.org

The Trustees of Reservations, 572 Essex St., Beverly, MA 01915, Tel. (978) 921-1944, web: www.thetrustees.org

IMBA Rules of the Trail

1. Ride on open trails only.
2. Leave no trace.
3. Control your bicycle.
4. Always yield trail.
5. Never spook animals.
6. Plan ahead.

*Take only pictures and memories
and leave only waffle prints.*

To receive the following books send check or money order,
plus 5% sales tax for Massachusetts residents, to:

Active Publications
P.O. Box 1037
Concord, MA 01742-1037

Number of copies:

_____*Mountain Biking Near Boston* ($15.95)

_____*Mountain Biking New Hampshire* ($12.95)

_____*Bike Paths of Massachusetts* ($13.95)

Name: _____

Address:_____

_____ZIP_____

RIDE THE TRAILS!
... SAVE THE TRAILS!

What were all about...

NEMBA is a non-profit organization of mountain bikers who enjoy to ride on and take care of New England trails. With thousands of members all around New England, NEMBA has many programs designed to create a link between recreation and conservation. We also have a lot of fun!

Giving back to the trails...

NEMBA's primary goal is to give back to the trails. We do this by holding many trail maintenance events around New England to repair trails and build new ones. We also have bicycle patrols to educate and assist all trails users, as well as educational booths which help spread the word about responsible mountain biking and the trail preservation.

New England Mountain Bike Association

NEMBA's Ride Series

NEMBA offers hundreds of mountain bike rides throughout New England for every level of rider, from beginner to expert. We also offer family rides, women's rides and hardcore all-day epics! NEMBA rides are led by NEMBA members for our members! Join us to find the best singletrack around!

SingleTracks, NEMBA's Magazine

All members receive a year's worth of our 40 page magazine with features, entertainment and the latest about the New England mountain bike scene.

The New England Mountain Bike Association

WWW.NEMBA.ORG   800-576-3622
Membership is tax-deductible!